egg s[illegible]y

私は準備ができている。
Hello.
I am ready.

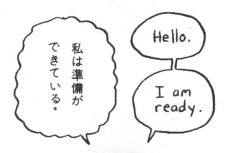

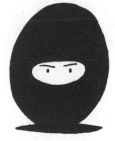

by J. Marc Schmidt

Published by SLG Publishing

President & Publisher
Dan Vado

Editor-in-Chief
Jennifer de Guzman

Director of Sales
Deb Moskyok

Production Assistant
Eleanor Lawson

SLG Publishing
P.O. Box 26427
San Jose, CA 95113

www.slavelabor.com

First Printing: July 2004
ISBN 0-943151-94-5

Egg Story is ™ and © 2004 J. Marc Schmidt, all
rights reserved. No part of this publication may
be reproduced without the permission of J. Marc
Schmidt and SLG Publishing, except for purposes
of review. Printed in Canada.

1

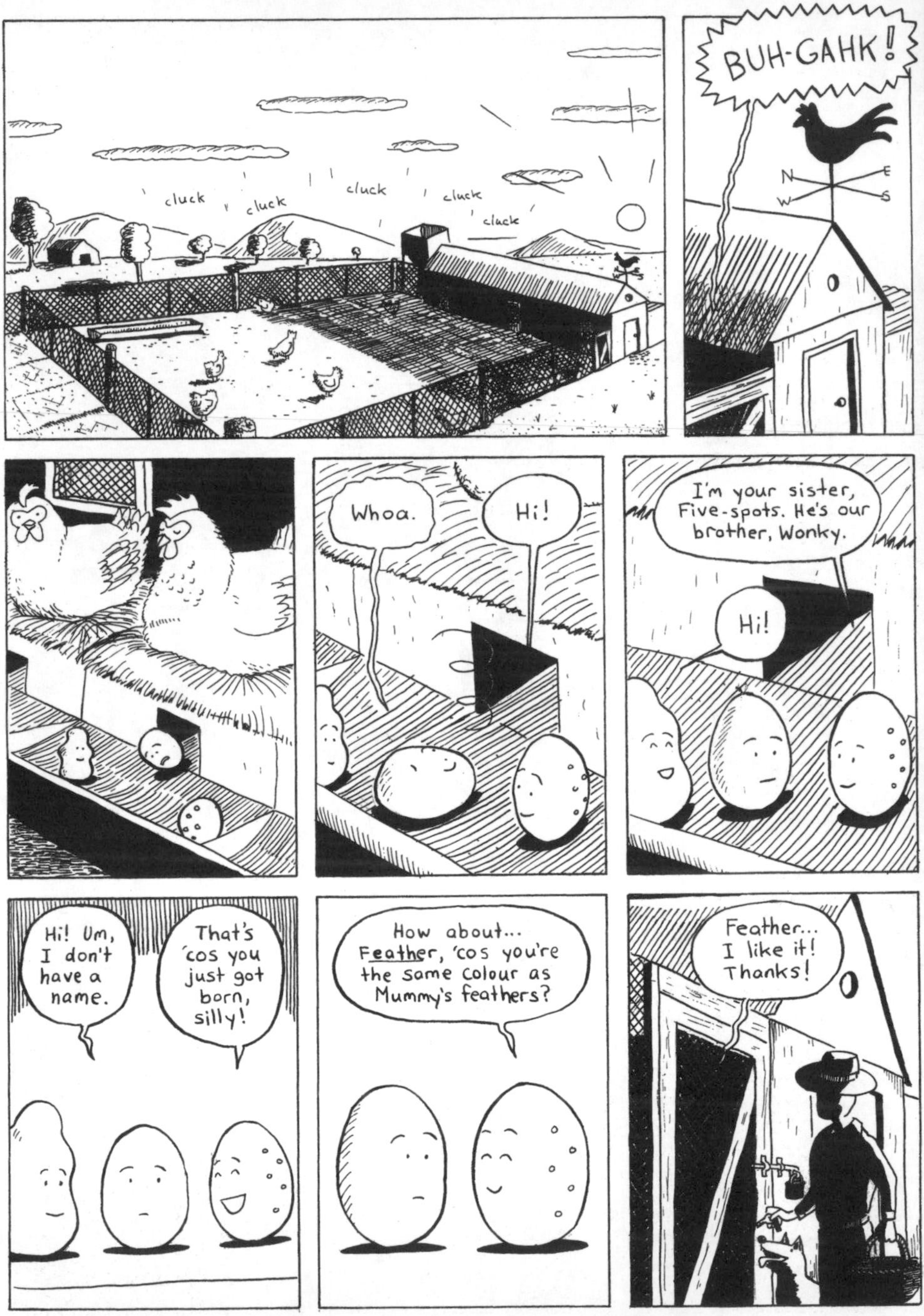
cluck
cluck
cluck
cluck
cluck
BUH-GAHK!
N
E
W
S
Whoa.
Hi!
I'm your sister, Five-spots. He's our brother, Wonky.
Hi!
Hi! Um, I don't have a name.
That's 'cos you just got born, silly!
How about... Feather, 'cos you're the same colour as Mummy's feathers?
Feather... I like it! Thanks!

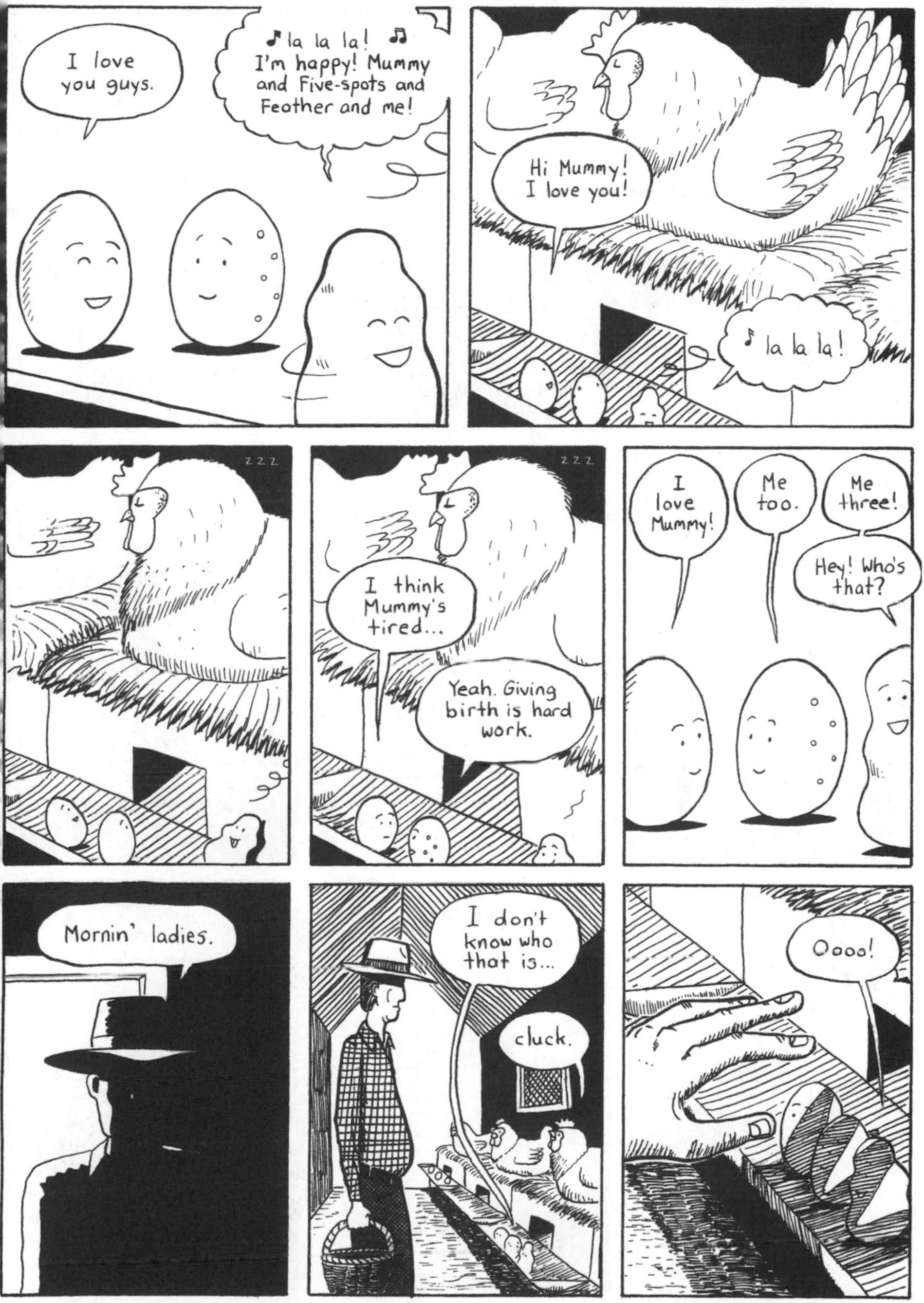
I love you guys.
♪ la la la! ♫ I'm happy! Mummy and Five-spots and Feather and me!
Hi Mummy! I love you!
♪ la la la!
z z z
z z z
I think Mummy's tired...
Yeah. Giving birth is hard work.
I love Mummy!
Me too.
Me three!
Hey! Who's that?
Mornin' ladies.
I don't know who that is...
cluck.
Oooo!

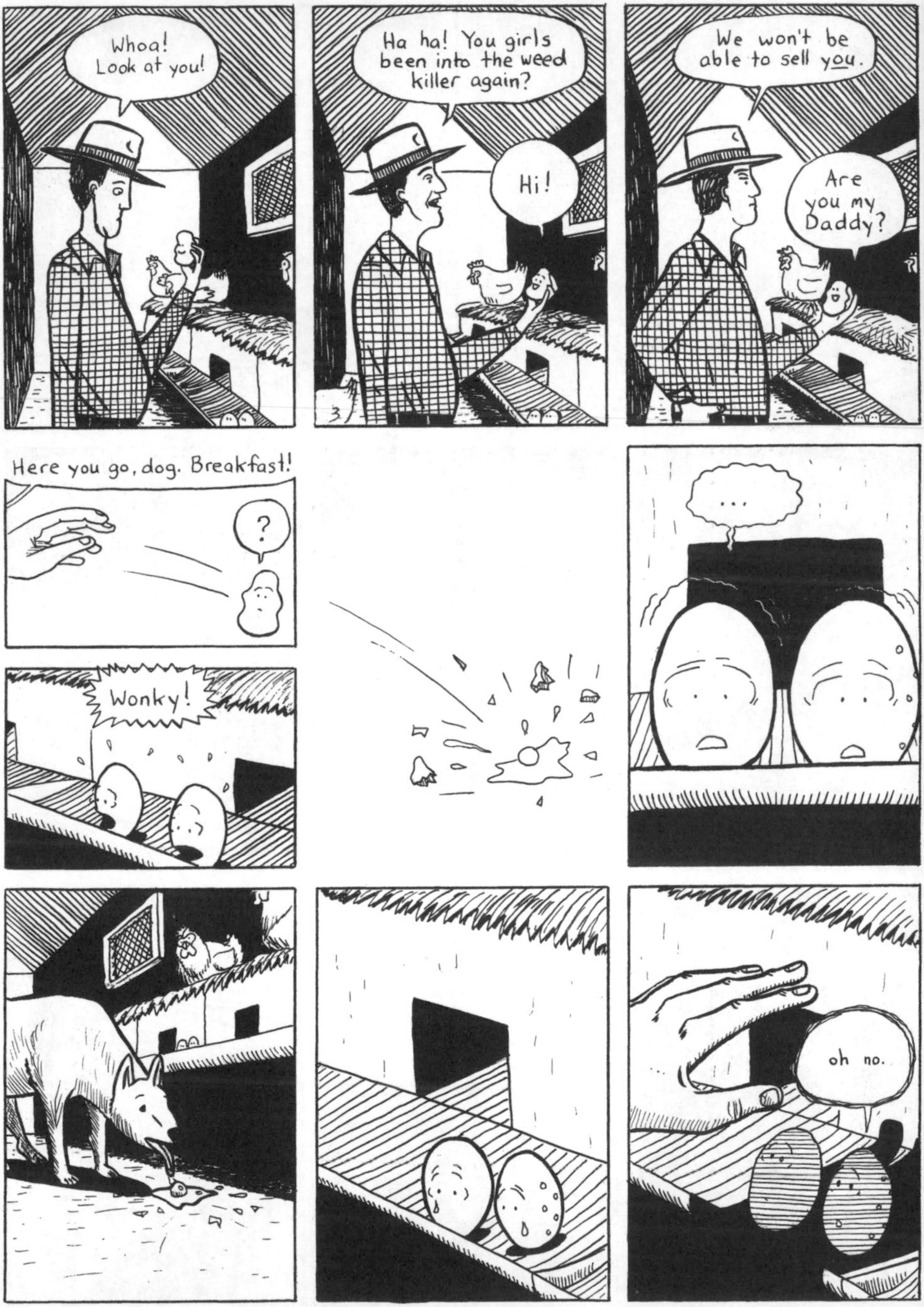
Whoa! Look at you!
Ha ha! You girls been into the weed killer again?
Hi!
We won't be able to sell you.
Are you my Daddy?
Here you go, dog. Breakfast!
?
Wonky!
...
oh no.

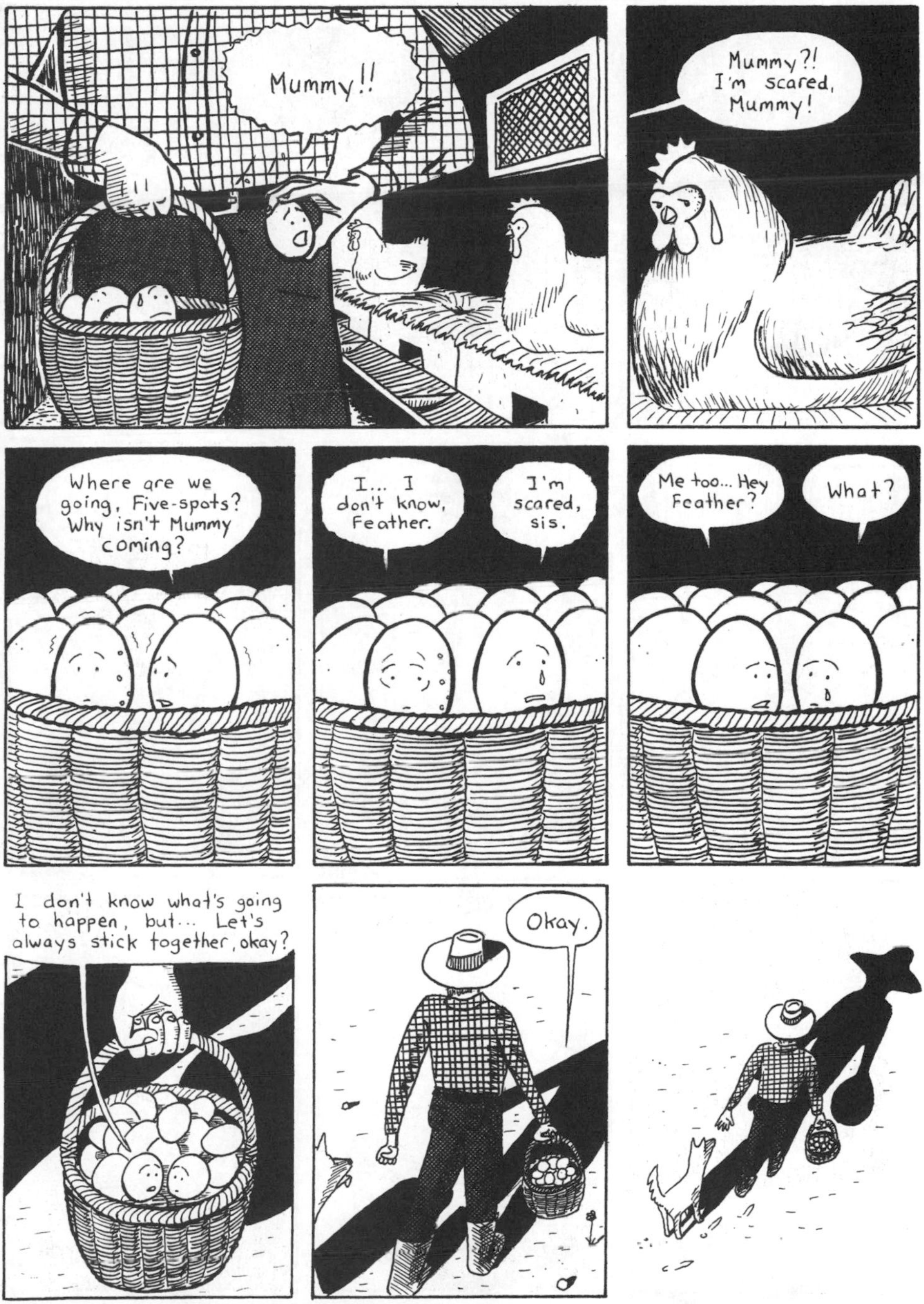
Mummy!!
Mummy?! I'm scared, Mummy!
Where are we going, Five-spots? Why isn't Mummy coming?
I... I don't know, Feather.
I'm scared, sis.
Me too... Hey Feather?
What?
I don't know what's going to happen, but... Let's always stick together, okay?
Okay.

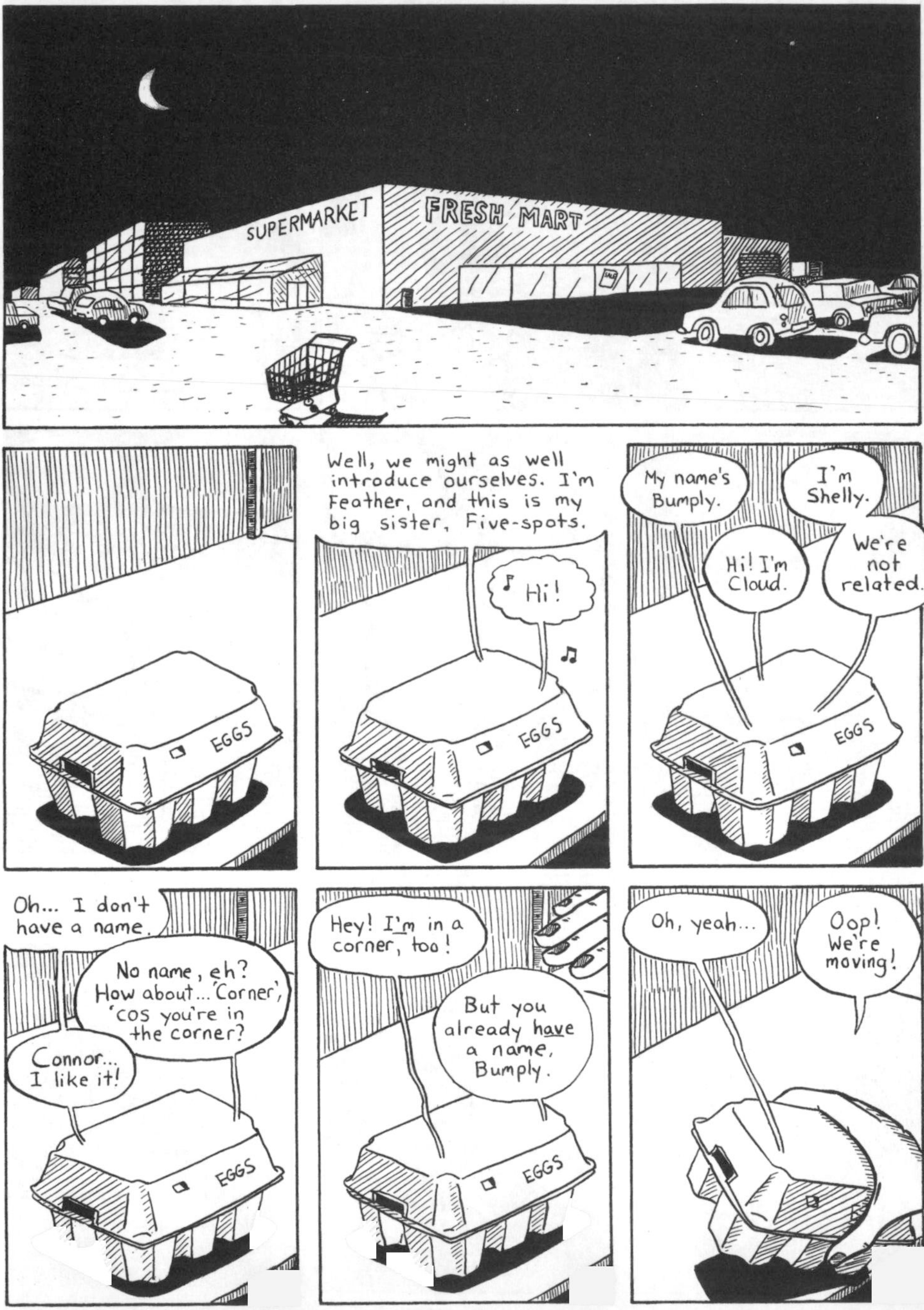
SUPERMARKET
FRESH MART
SALE
Well, we might as well introduce ourselves. I'm Feather, and this is my big sister, Five-spots.
Hi!
My name's Bumply.
Hi! I'm Cloud.
I'm Shelly.
We're not related.
Oh... I don't have a name.
No name, eh? How about... 'Corner', 'cos you're in the corner?
Connor... I like it!
Hey! I'm in a corner, too!
But you already have a name, Bumply.
Oh, yeah...
Oop! We're moving!
EGGS

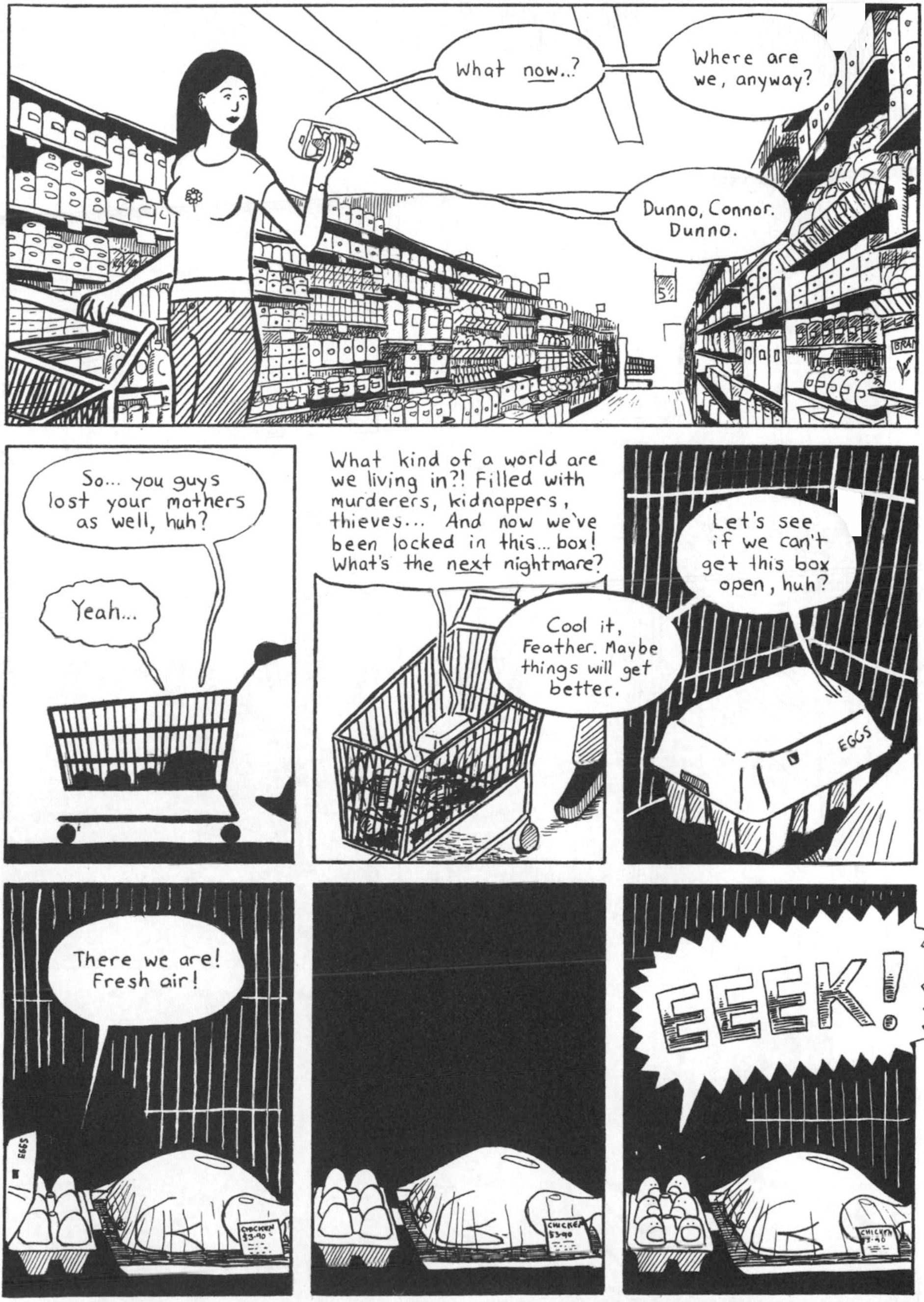

What now..?
Where are we, anyway?
Dunno, Connor. Dunno.
So... you guys lost your mothers as well, huh?
Yeah...
What kind of a world are we living in?! Filled with murderers, kidnappers, thieves... And now we've been locked in this... box! What's the next nightmare?
Cool it, Feather. Maybe things will get better.
Let's see if we can't get this box open, huh?
EGGS
There we are! Fresh air!
EGGS
CHICKEN $3.90
CHICKEN $3.90
EEEK!

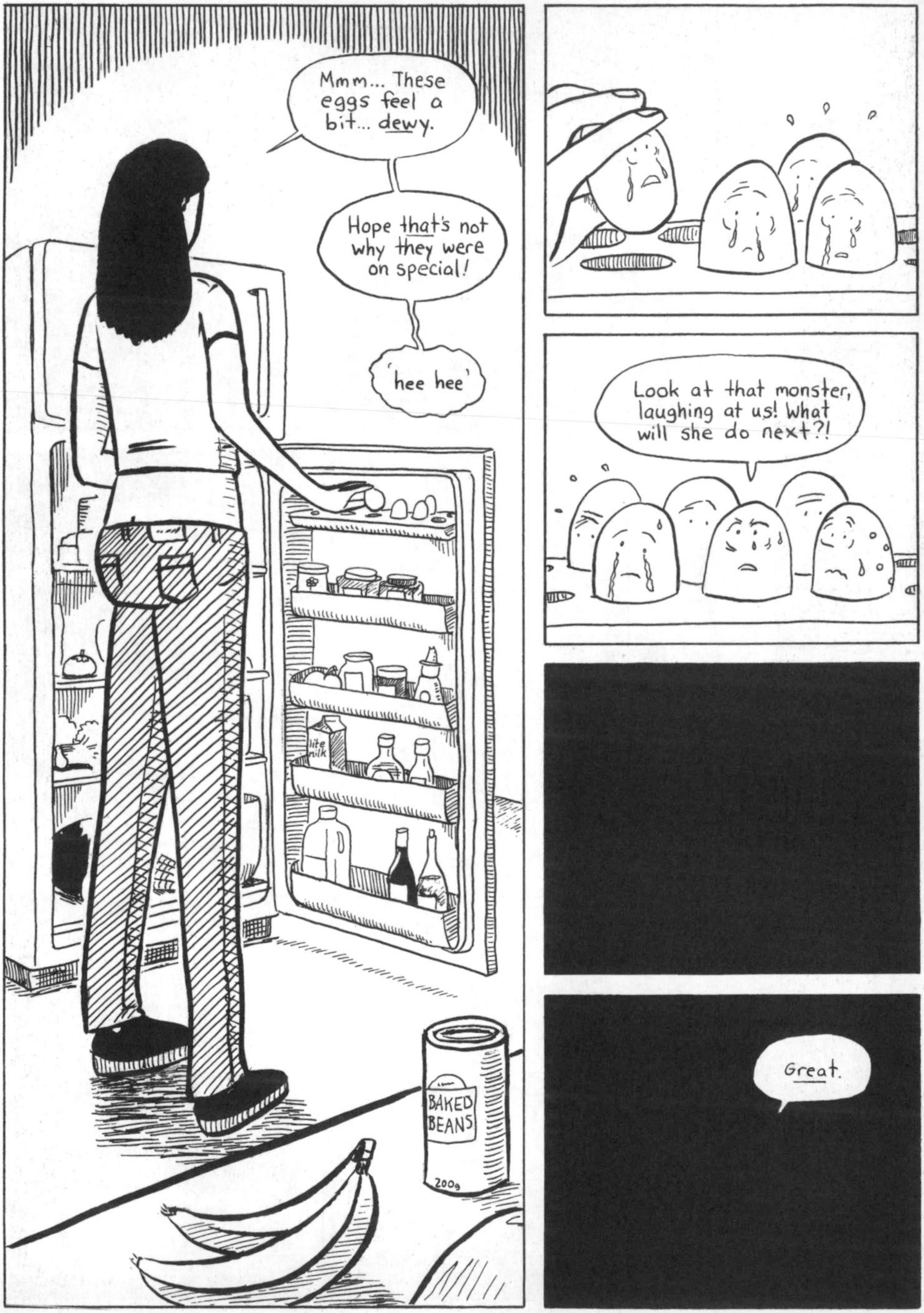
Mmm... These eggs feel a bit... dewy.
Hope that's not why they were on special!
'hee hee'
lite milk
BAKED BEANS
200g
Look at that monster, laughing at us! What will she do next?!
Great.

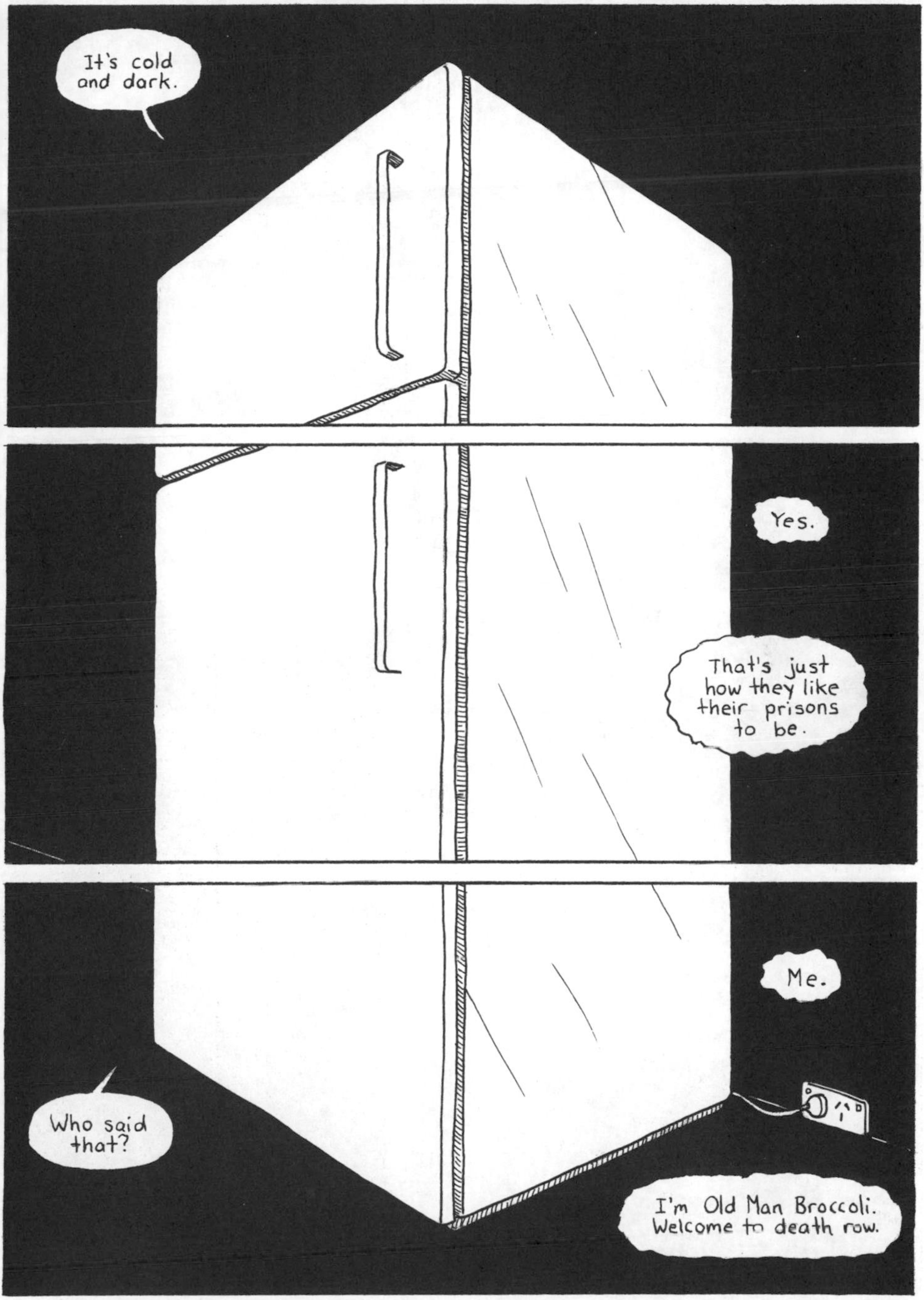
It's cold and dark.
Yes.
That's just how they like their prisons to be.
Me.
Who said that?
I'm Old Man Broccoli. Welcome to death row.

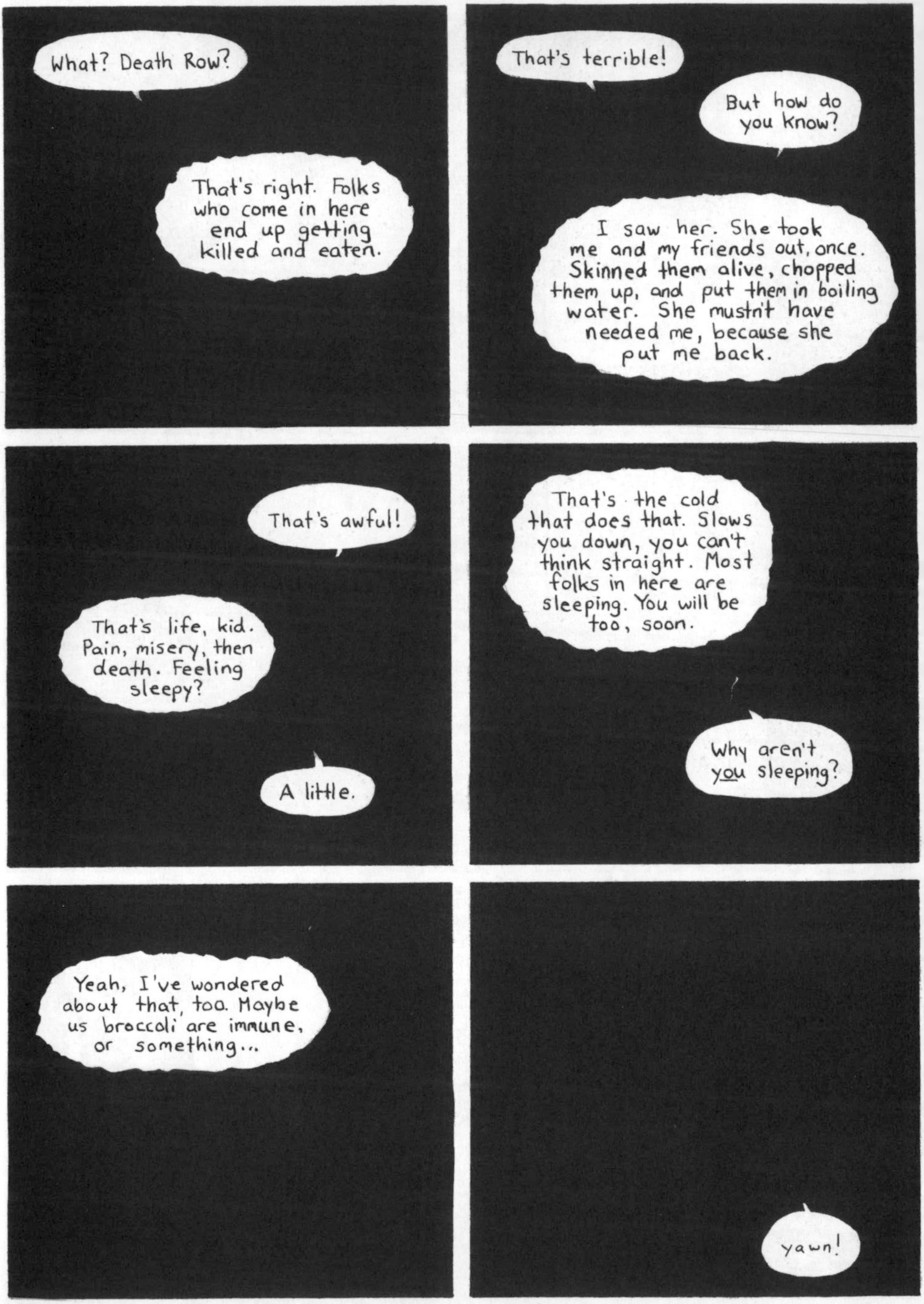
What? Death Row?
That's right. Folks who come in here end up getting killed and eaten.
That's terrible!
But how do you know?
I saw her. She took me and my friends out, once. Skinned them alive, chopped them up, and put them in boiling water. She mustn't have needed me, because she put me back.
That's awful!
That's life, kid. Pain, misery, then death. Feeling sleepy?
A little.
That's the cold that does that. Slows you down, you can't think straight. Most folks in here are sleeping. You will be too, soon.
Why aren't you sleeping?
Yeah, I've wondered about that, too. Maybe us broccoli are immune, or something...
yawn!

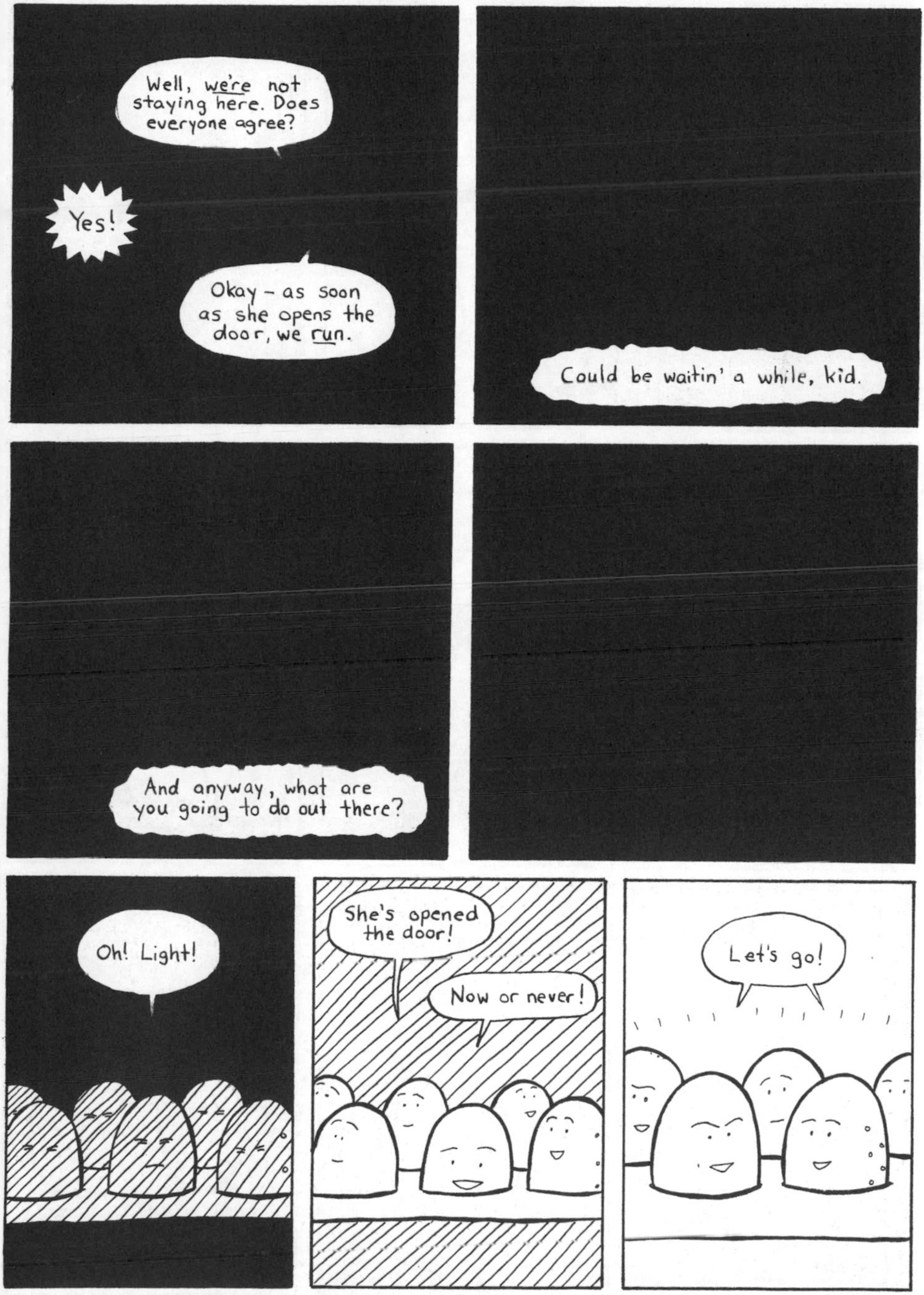

Well, we're not staying here. Does everyone agree?
Yes!
Okay – as soon as she opens the door, we run.
Could be waitin' a while, kid.
And anyway, what are you going to do out there?
Oh! Light!
She's opened the door!
Now or never!
Let's go!

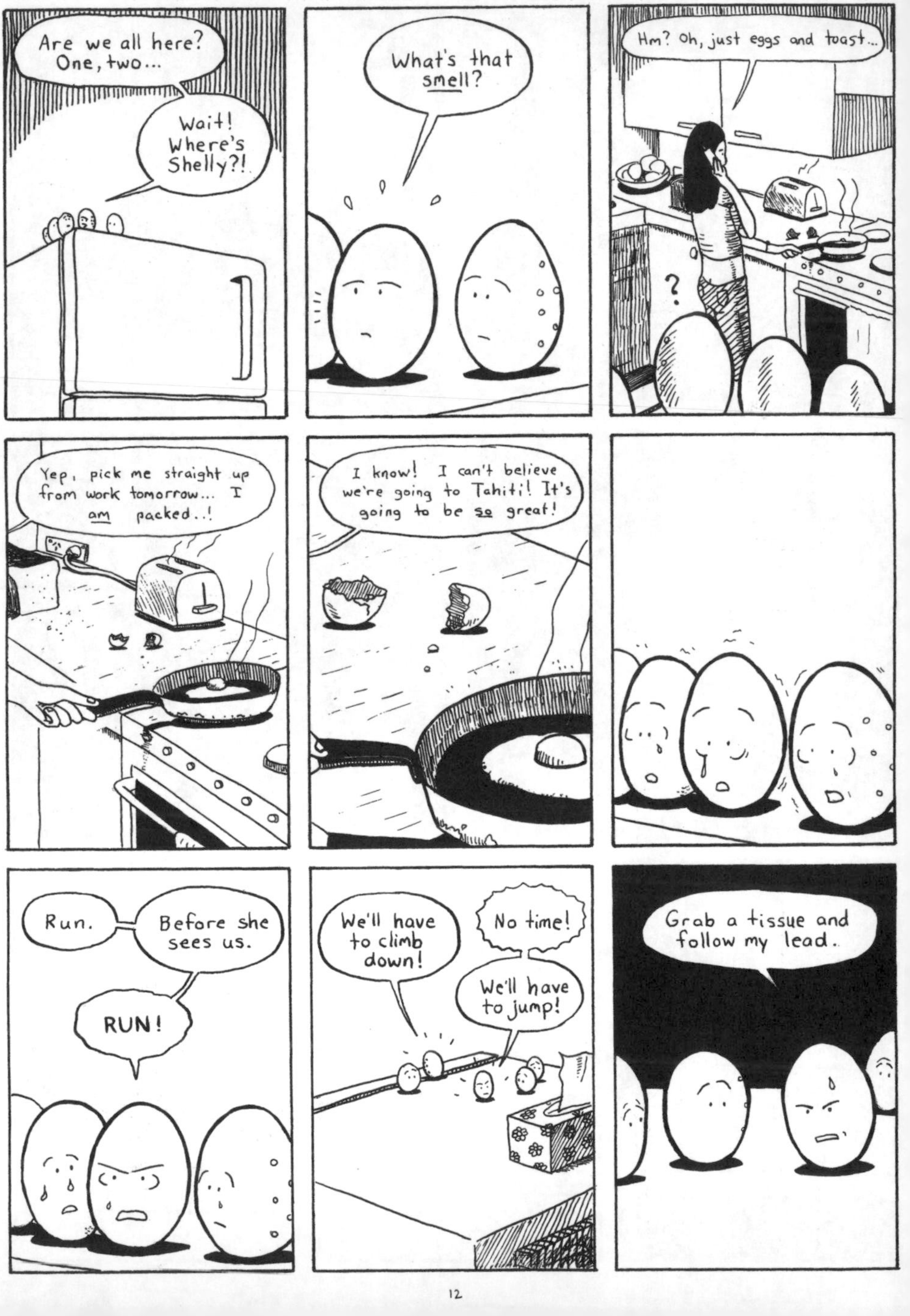
Are we all here? One, two...
Wait! Where's Shelly?!
What's that smell?
Hm? Oh, just eggs and toast...
Yep, pick me straight up from work tomorrow... I am packed..!
I know! I can't believe we're going to Tahiti! It's going to be so great!
Run.
Before she sees us.
RUN!
We'll have to climb down!
No time!
We'll have to jump!
Grab a tissue and follow my lead.

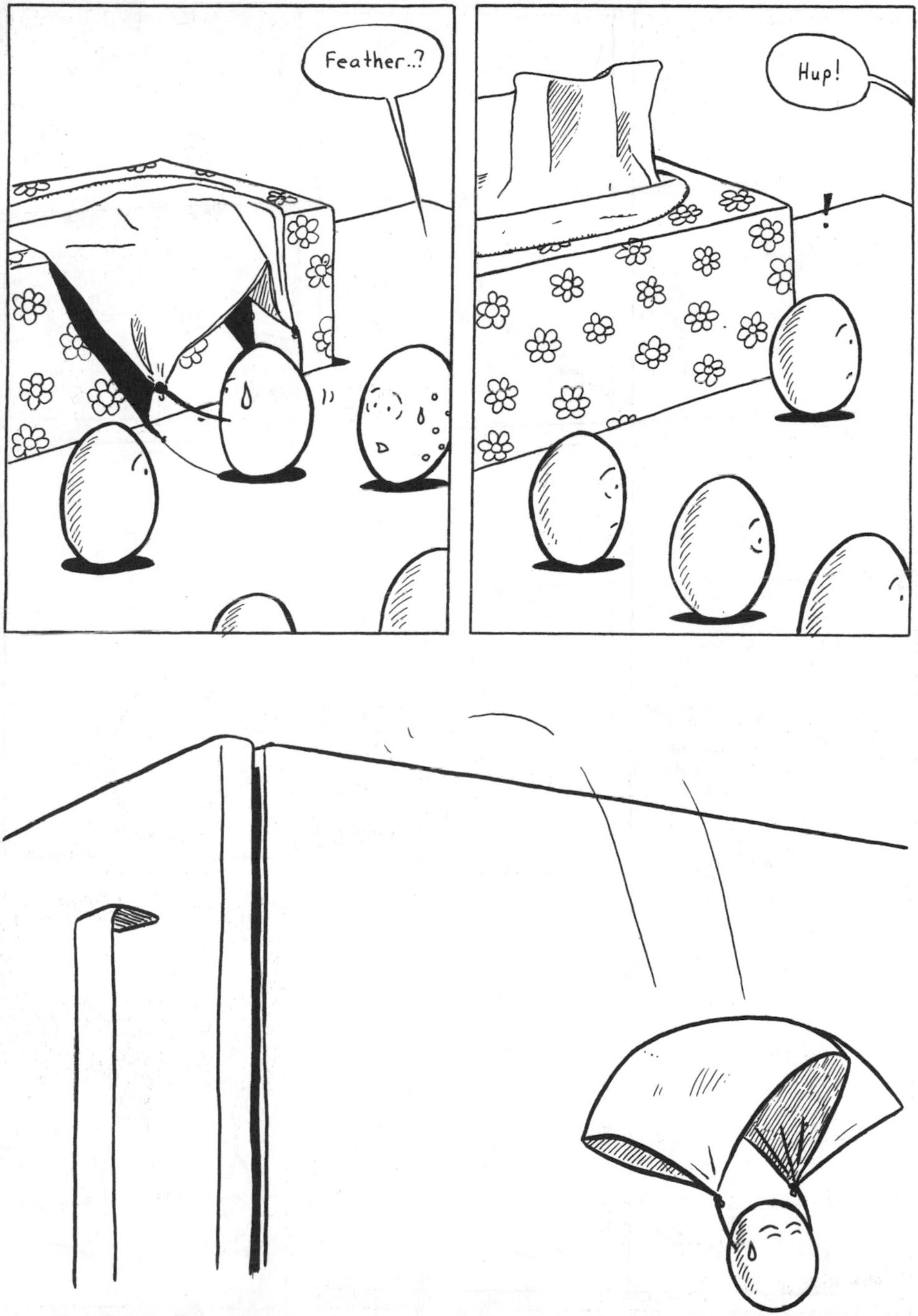
Feather..?
Hup!
!

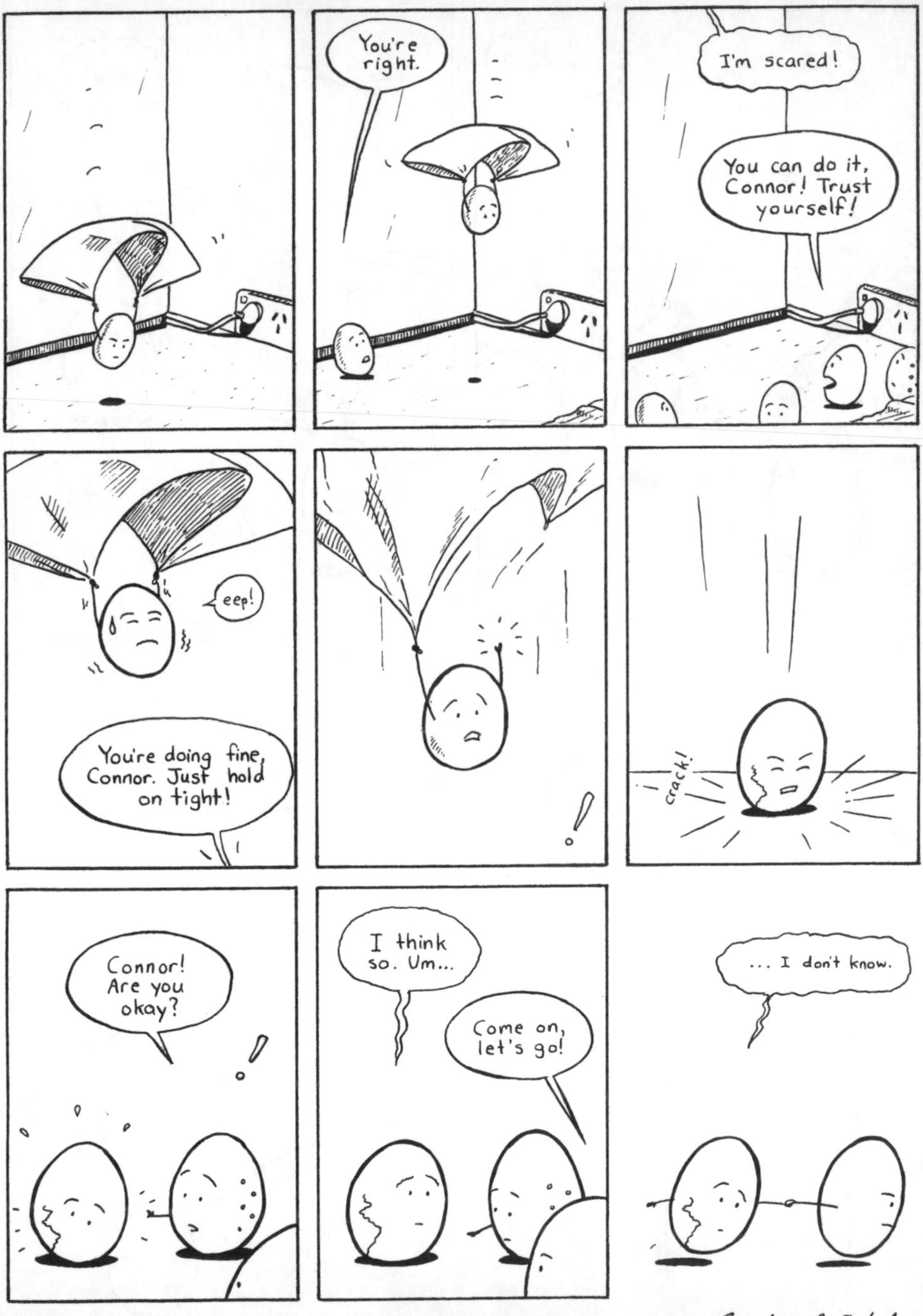
You're right.
I'm scared!
You can do it, Connor! Trust yourself!
eep!
You're doing fine, Connor. Just hold on tight!
!
crack!
Connor! Are you okay?
!
I think so. Um...
Come on, let's go!
... I don't know.

End of Act 1...

2

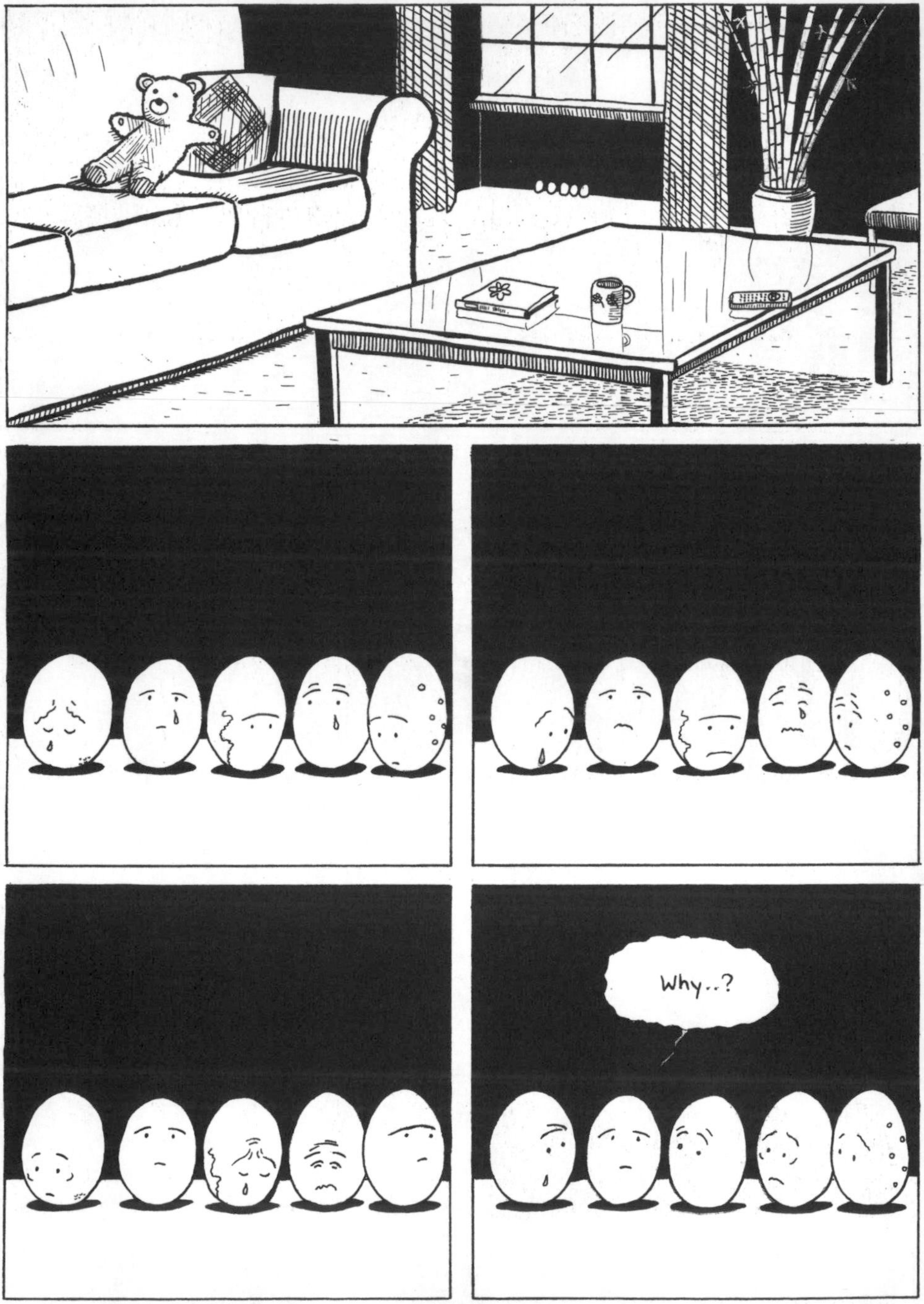
Why..?

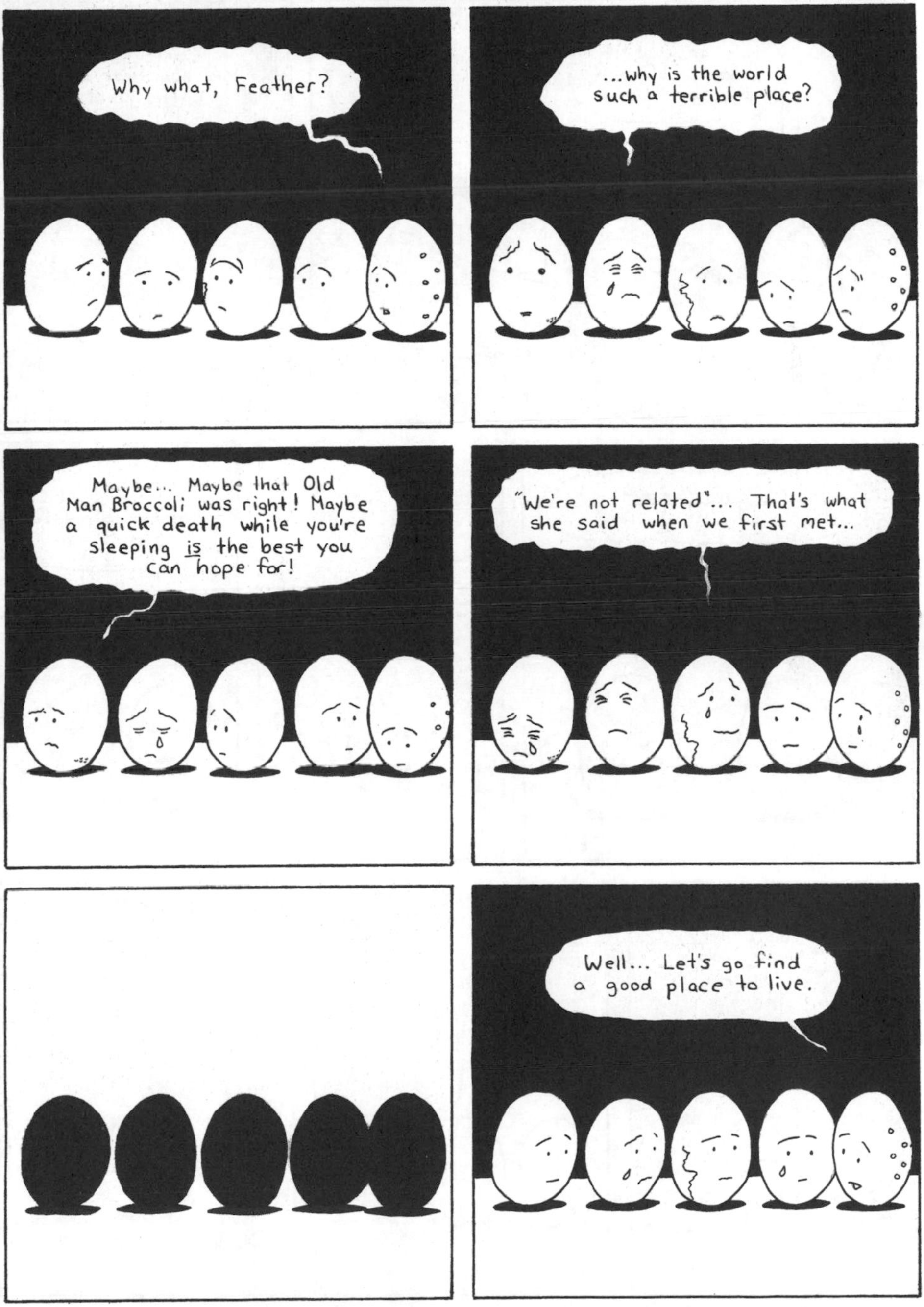
Why what, Feather?
...why is the world such a terrible place?
Maybe... Maybe that Old Man Broccoli was right! Maybe a quick death while you're sleeping is the best you can hope for!
"We're not related"... That's what she said when we first met...
Well... Let's go find a good place to live.

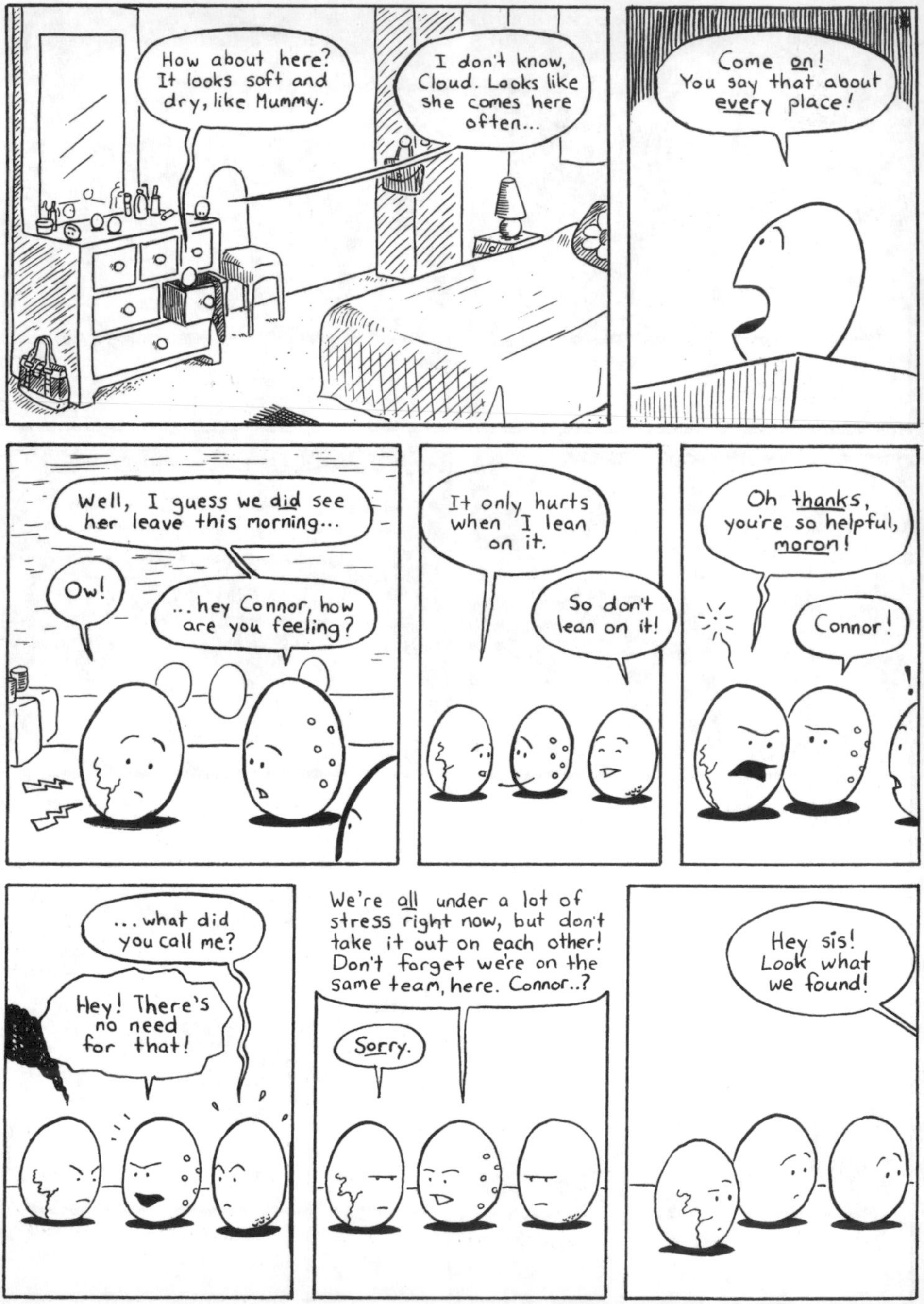

How about here? It looks soft and dry, like Mummy.
I don't know, Cloud. Looks like she comes here often...
Come on! You say that about every place!
Well, I guess we did see her leave this morning...
Ow!
...hey Connor, how are you feeling?
It only hurts when I lean on it.
So don't lean on it!
Oh thanks, you're so helpful, moron!
Connor!
...what did you call me?
Hey! There's no need for that!
We're all under a lot of stress right now, but don't take it out on each other! Don't forget we're on the same team, here. Connor..?
Sorry.
Hey sis! Look what we found!

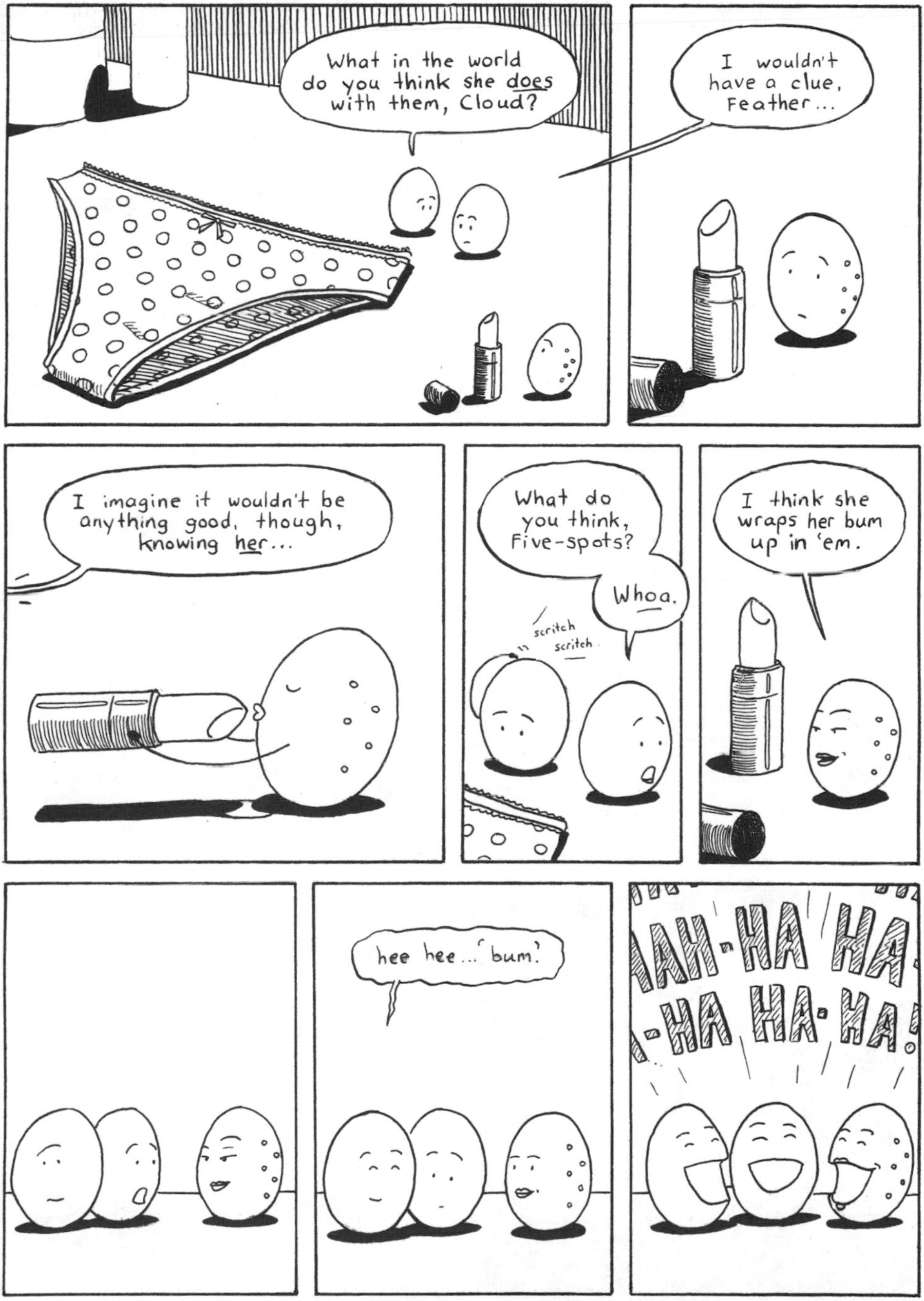
What in the world do you think she does with them, Cloud?
I wouldn't have a clue, Feather...
I imagine it wouldn't be anything good, though, knowing her...
What do you think, Five-spots?
Whoa.
scritch
scritch
I think she wraps her bum up in 'em.
hee hee... 'bum.'
AH-HA HA HA
HA HA-HA-HA!

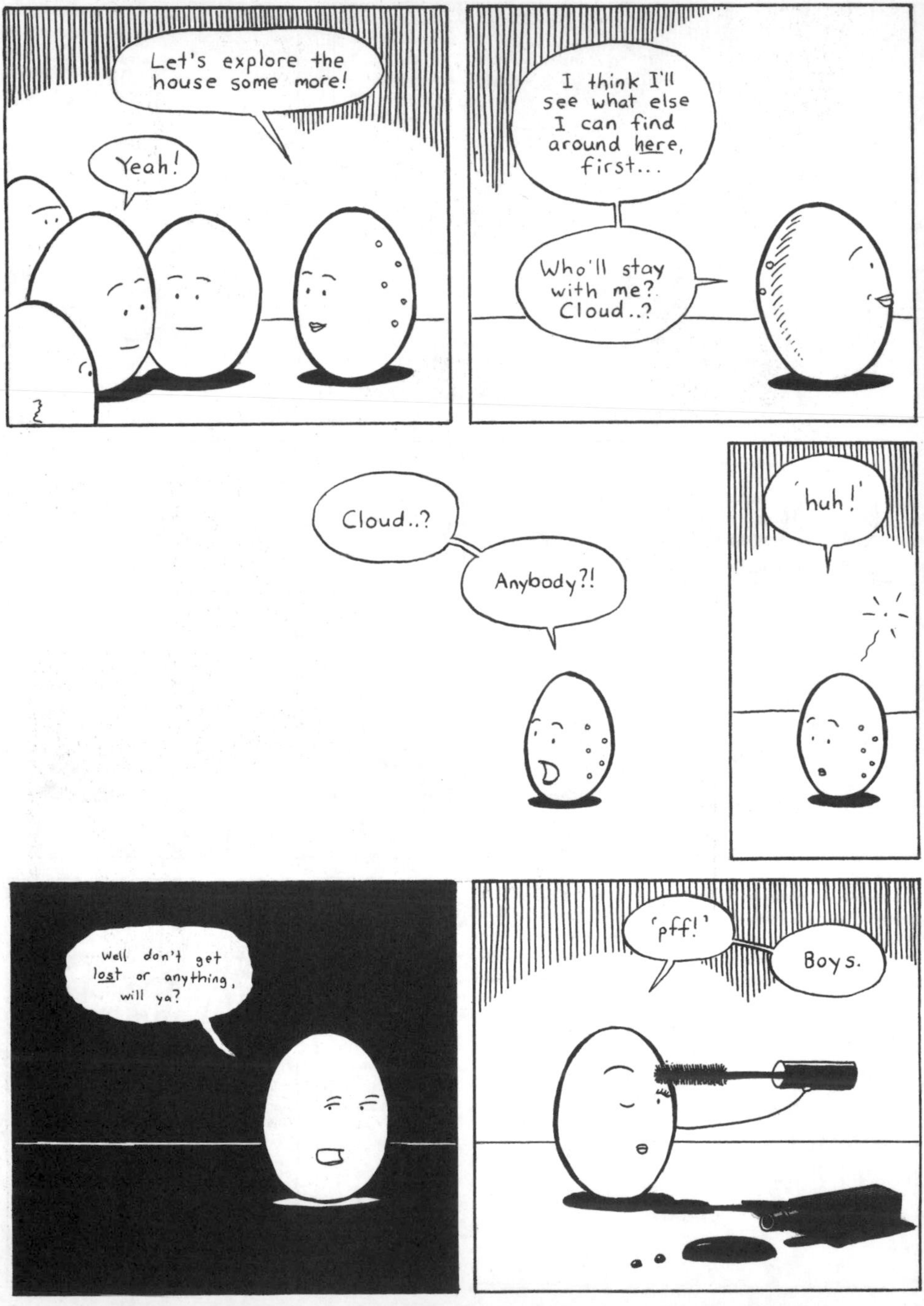

Let's explore the house some more!
Yeah!
I think I'll see what else I can find around here, first...
Who'll stay with me? Cloud..?
Cloud..?
Anybody?!
'huh!'
Well don't get lost or anything, will ya?
'pff!'
Boys.

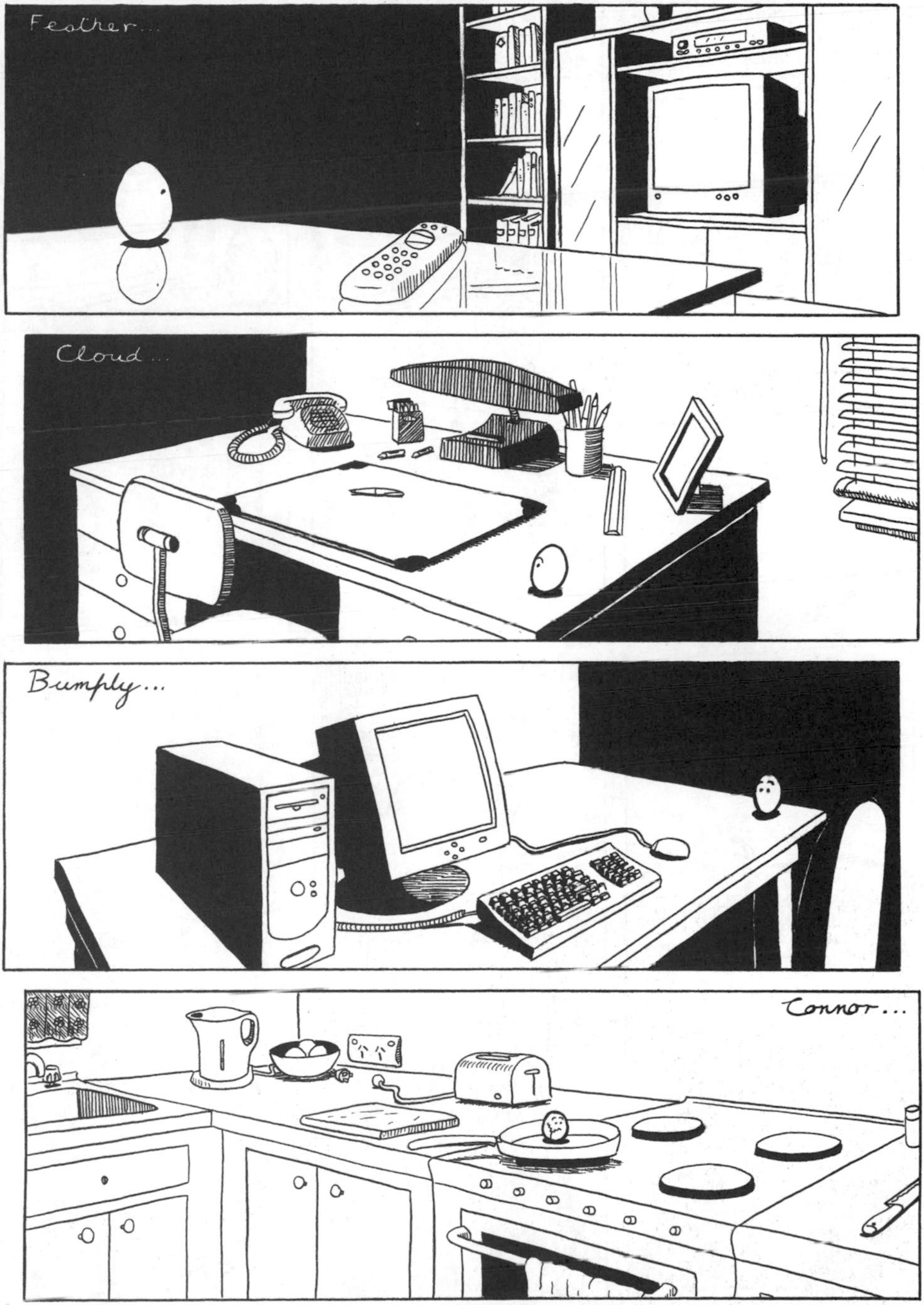
Feather...
Cloud...
Bumply...
Connor...

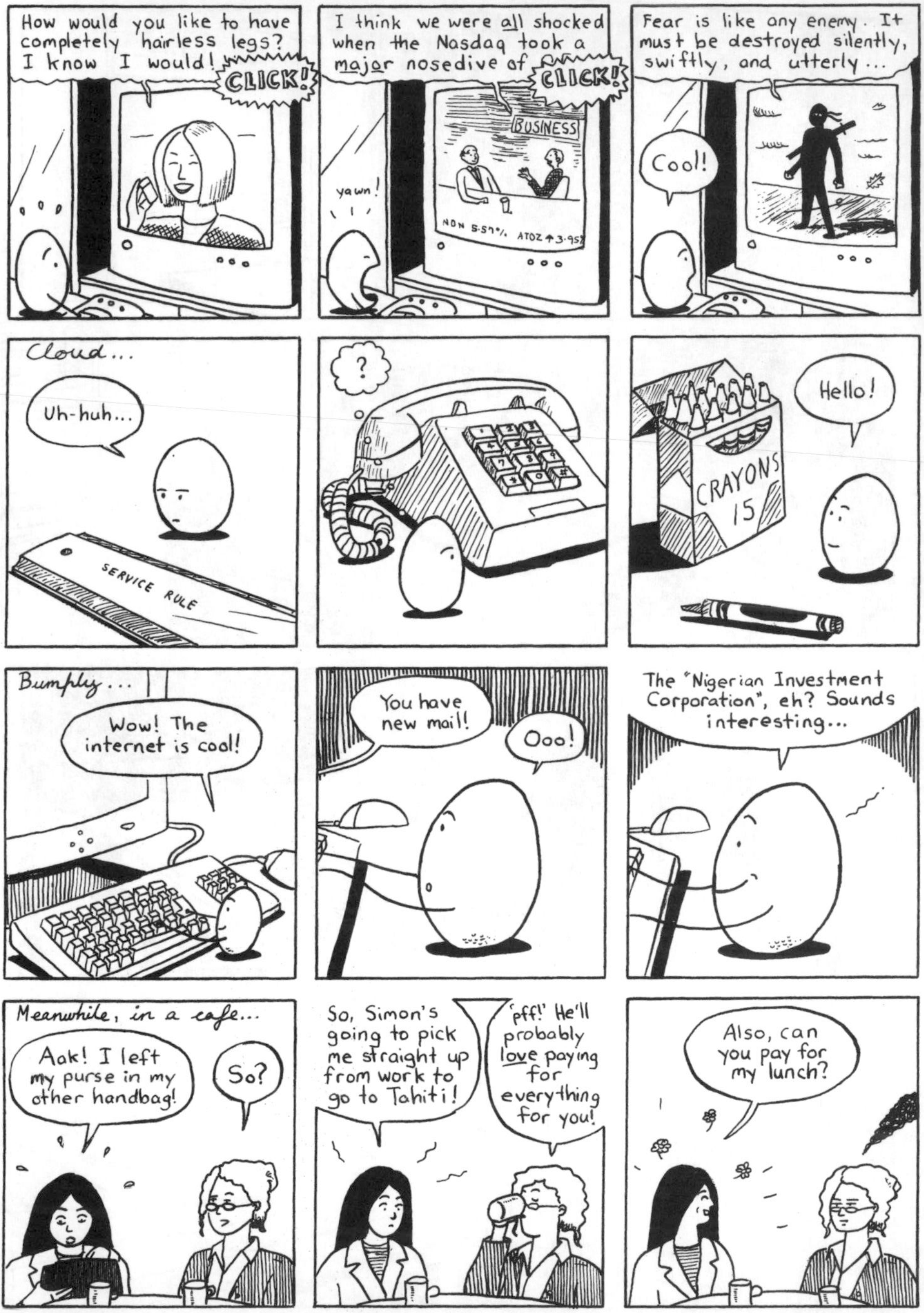
How would you like to have completely hairless legs? I know I would!
CLICK!
I think we were all shocked when the Nasdaq took a major nosedive of
CLICK!
BUSINESS
NDN 5.57%. ATOZ ↑ 3.95%
yawn!
Fear is like any enemy. It must be destroyed silently, swiftly, and utterly...
Cool!
Cloud...
Uh-huh...
SERVICE RULE
?
Hello!
CRAYONS 15
Bumply...
Wow! The internet is cool!
You have new mail!
Ooo!
The "Nigerian Investment Corporation", eh? Sounds interesting...
Meanwhile, in a cafe...
Aak! I left my purse in my other handbag!
So?
So, Simon's going to pick me straight up from work to go to Tahiti!
'pff!' He'll probably love paying for everything for you!
Also, can you pay for my lunch?

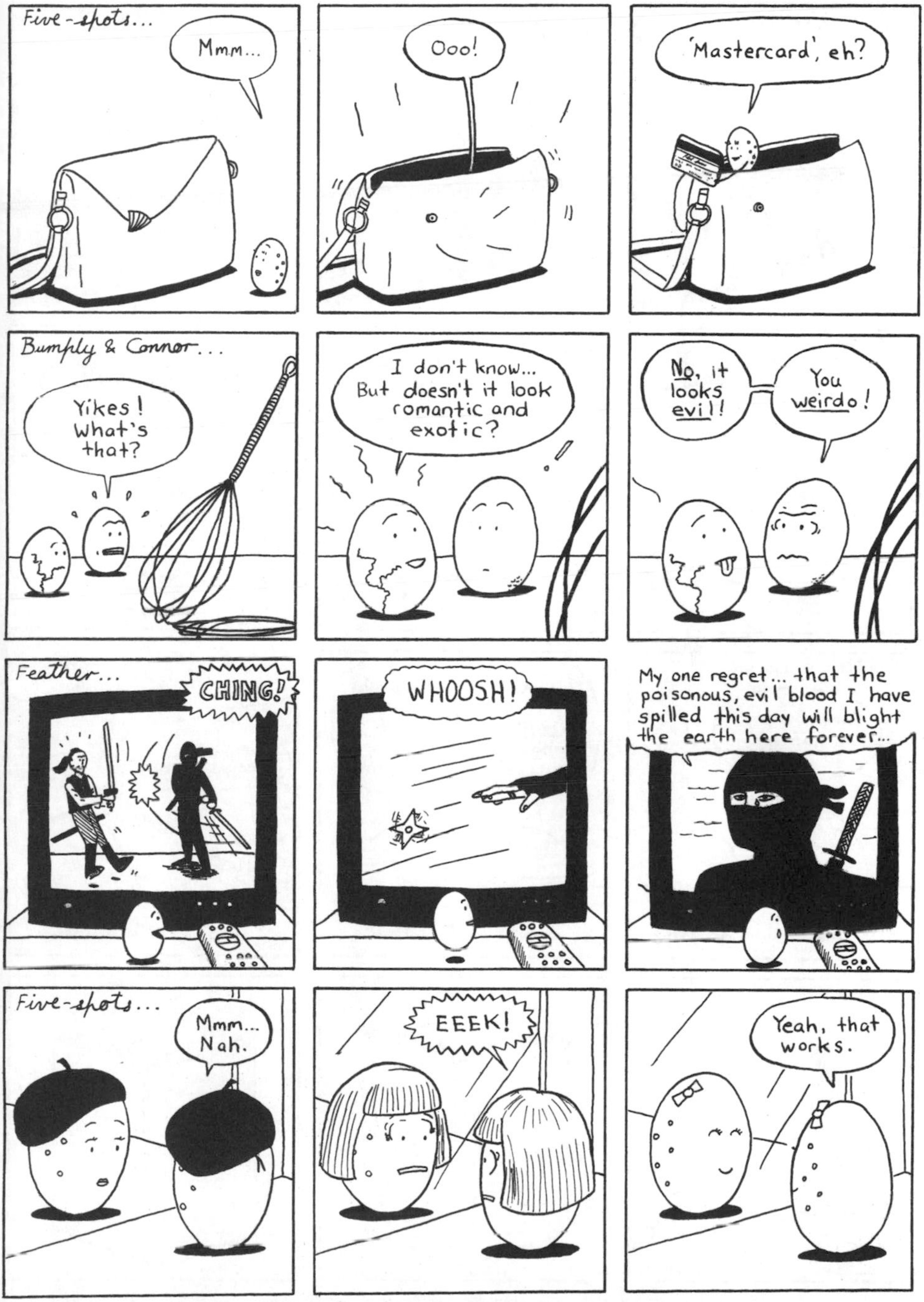
Five-spots...
Mmm...
Ooo!
'Mastercard', eh?
Bumply & Connor...
Yikes! What's that?
I don't know... But doesn't it look romantic and exotic?
No, it looks evil!
You weirdo!
Feather...
CHING!
WHOOSH!
My one regret... that the poisonous, evil blood I have spilled this day will blight the earth here forever...
Five-spots...
Mmm... Nah.
EEEK!
Yeah, that works.

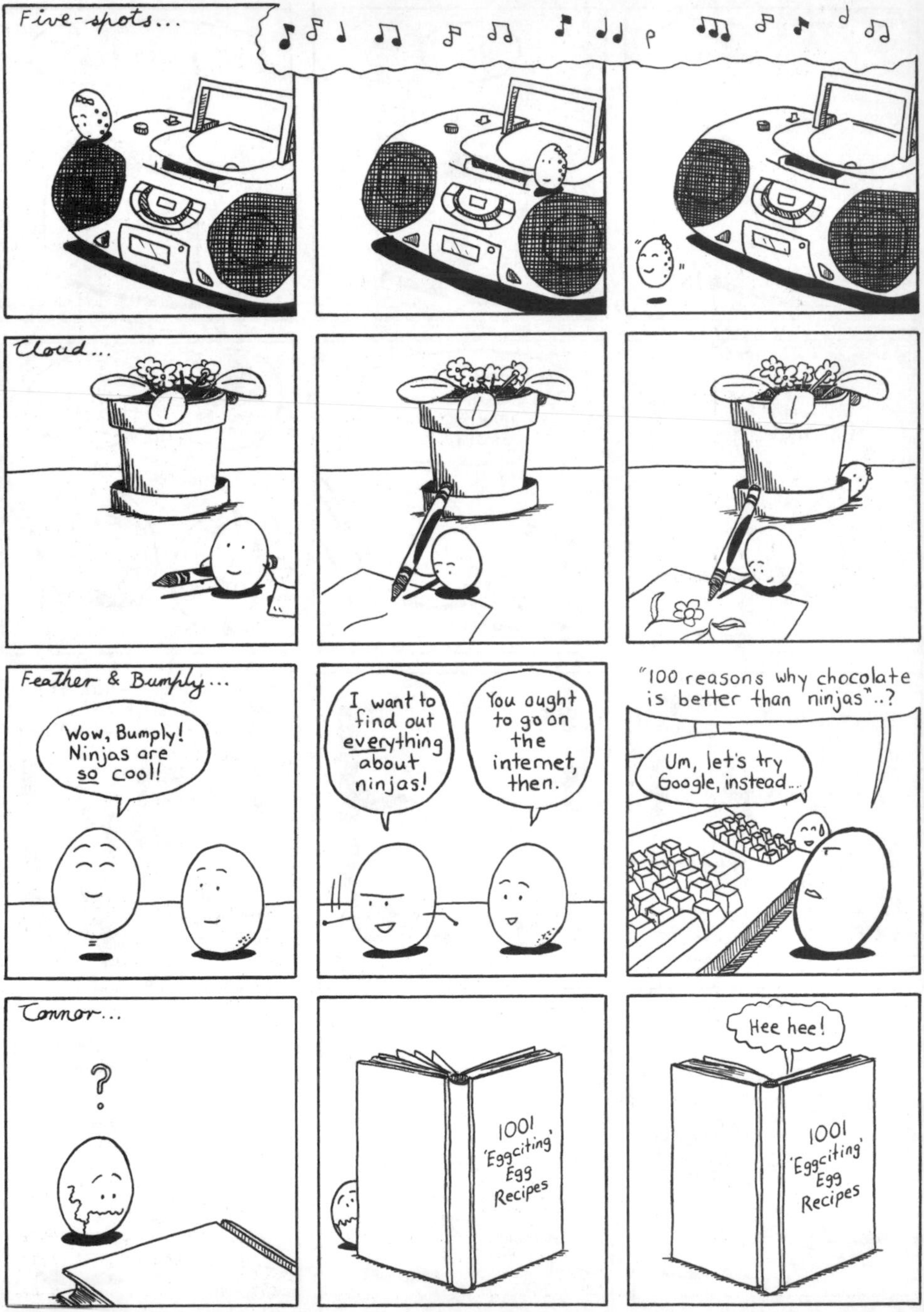
Five-spots...
Cloud...
Feather & Bumply...
Wow, Bumply! Ninjas are so cool!
I want to find out everything about ninjas!
You ought to go on the internet, then.
"100 reasons why chocolate is better than ninjas"..?
Um, let's try Google, instead...
Connor...
?
1001 'Eggciting' Egg Recipes
1001 'Eggciting' Egg Recipes
Hee hee!

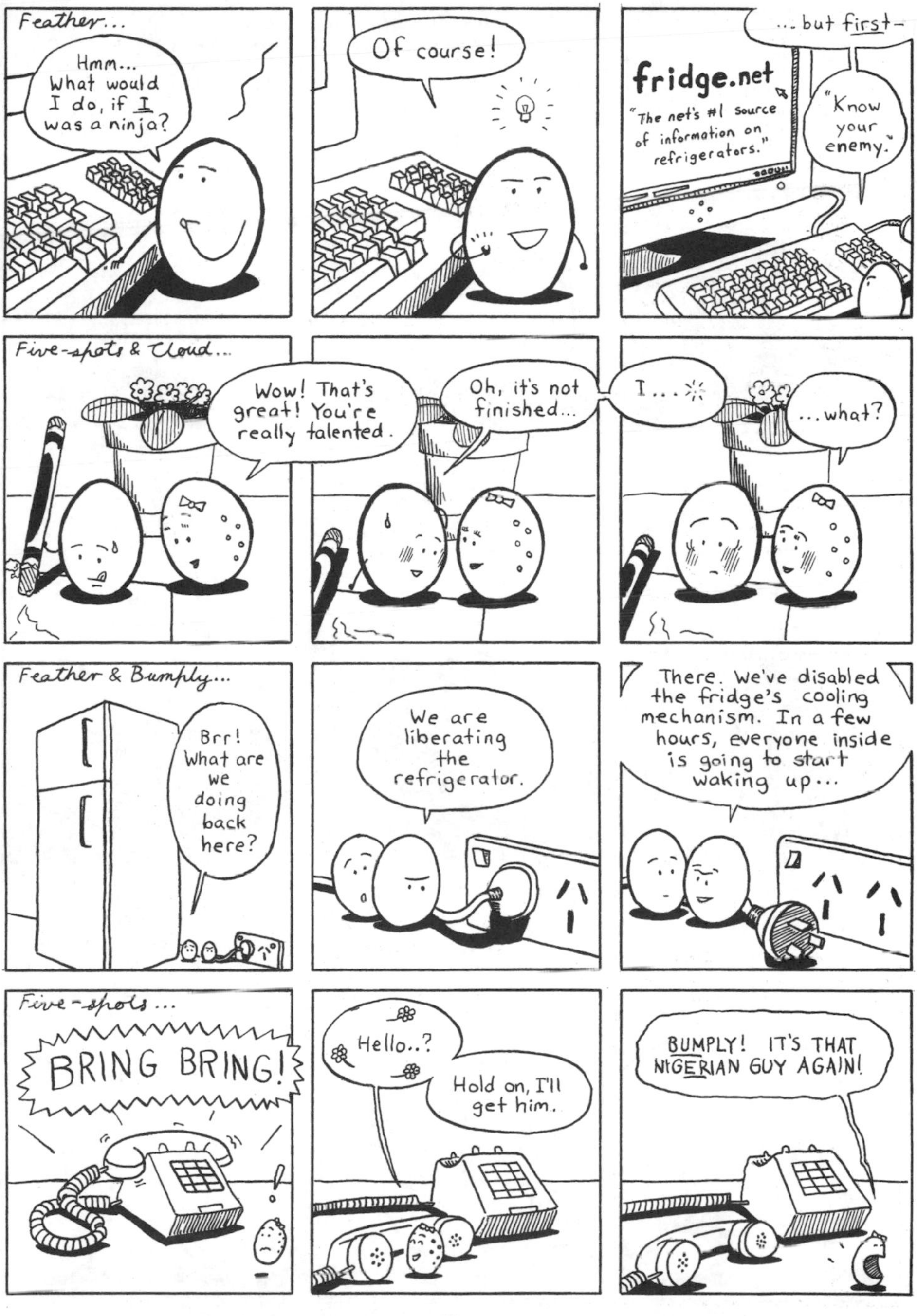
Feather...
Hmm... What would I do, if I was a ninja?
Of course!
fridge.net
"The net's #1 source of information on refrigerators."
... but first-
"Know your enemy."
Five-spots & Cloud...
Wow! That's great! You're really talented.
Oh, it's not finished...
I...
...what?
Feather & Bumply...
Brr! What are we doing back here?
We are liberating the refrigerator.
There. We've disabled the fridge's cooling mechanism. In a few hours, everyone inside is going to start waking up...
Five-spots...
BRING BRING!
Hello..?
Hold on, I'll get him.
BUMPLY! IT'S THAT NIGERIAN GUY AGAIN!

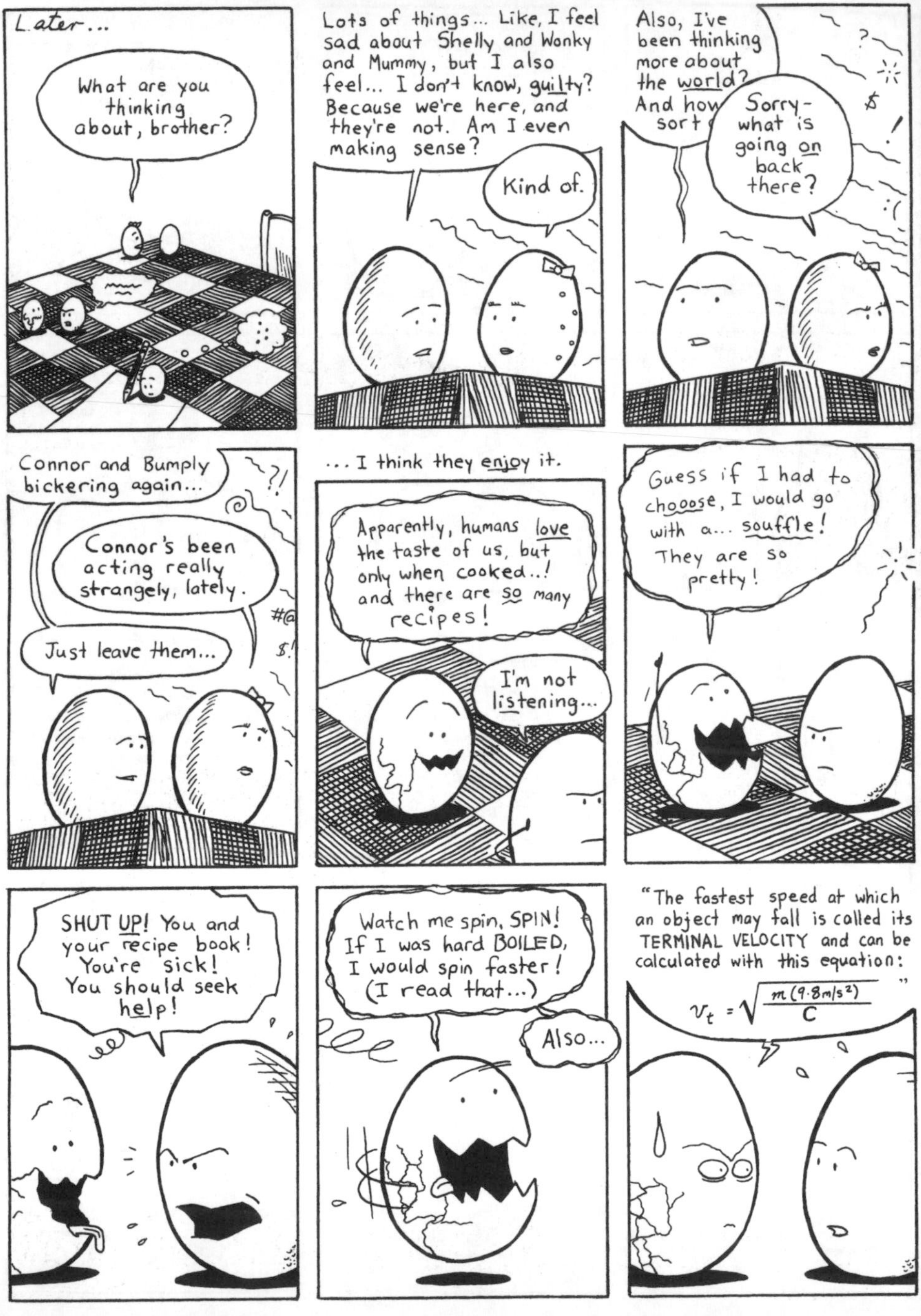
Later...
What are you thinking about, brother?
Lots of things... Like, I feel sad about Shelly and Wonky and Mummy, but I also feel... I don't know, guilty? Because we're here, and they're not. Am I even making sense?
Kind of.
Also, I've been thinking more about the world? And how
sort
Sorry- what is going on back there?
Connor and Bumply bickering again...
Connor's been acting really strangely, lately.
Just leave them...
?!
#@
$!
... I think they enjoy it.
Apparently, humans love the taste of us, but only when cooked...! and there are so many recipes!
I'm not listening...
Guess if I had to chooose, I would go with a... souffle! They are so pretty!
SHUT UP! You and your recipe book! You're sick! You should seek help!
Watch me spin, SPIN! If I was hard BOILED, I would spin faster! (I read that...)
Also...
"The fastest speed at which an object may fall is called its TERMINAL VELOCITY and can be calculated with this equation:
$v_t = \sqrt{\frac{m(9.8 m/s^2)}{C}}$"

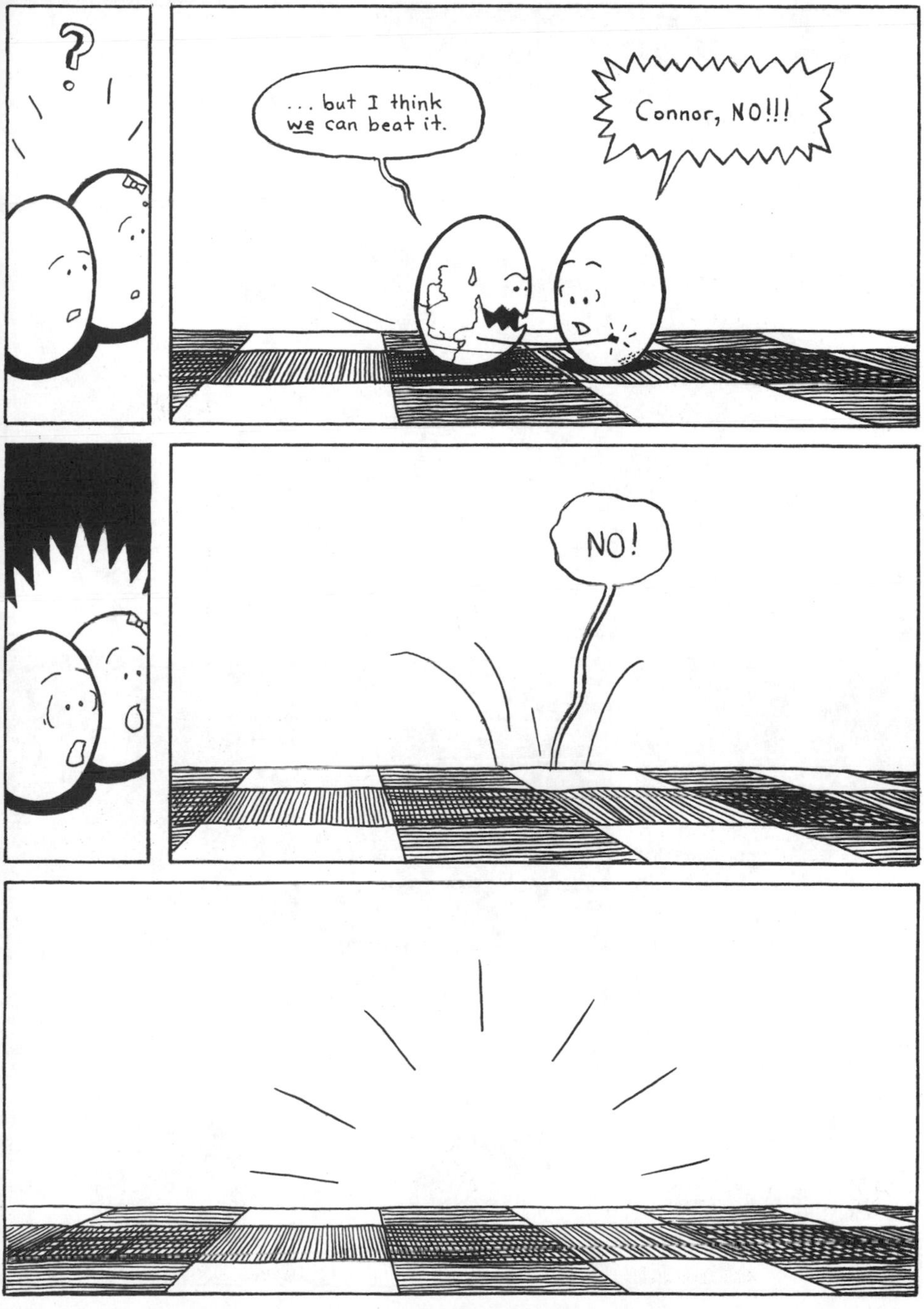
?
... but I think we can beat it.
Connor, NO!!!
NO!

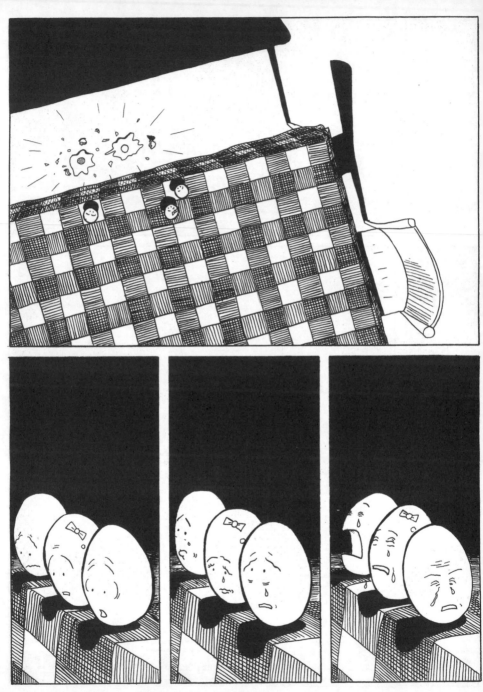

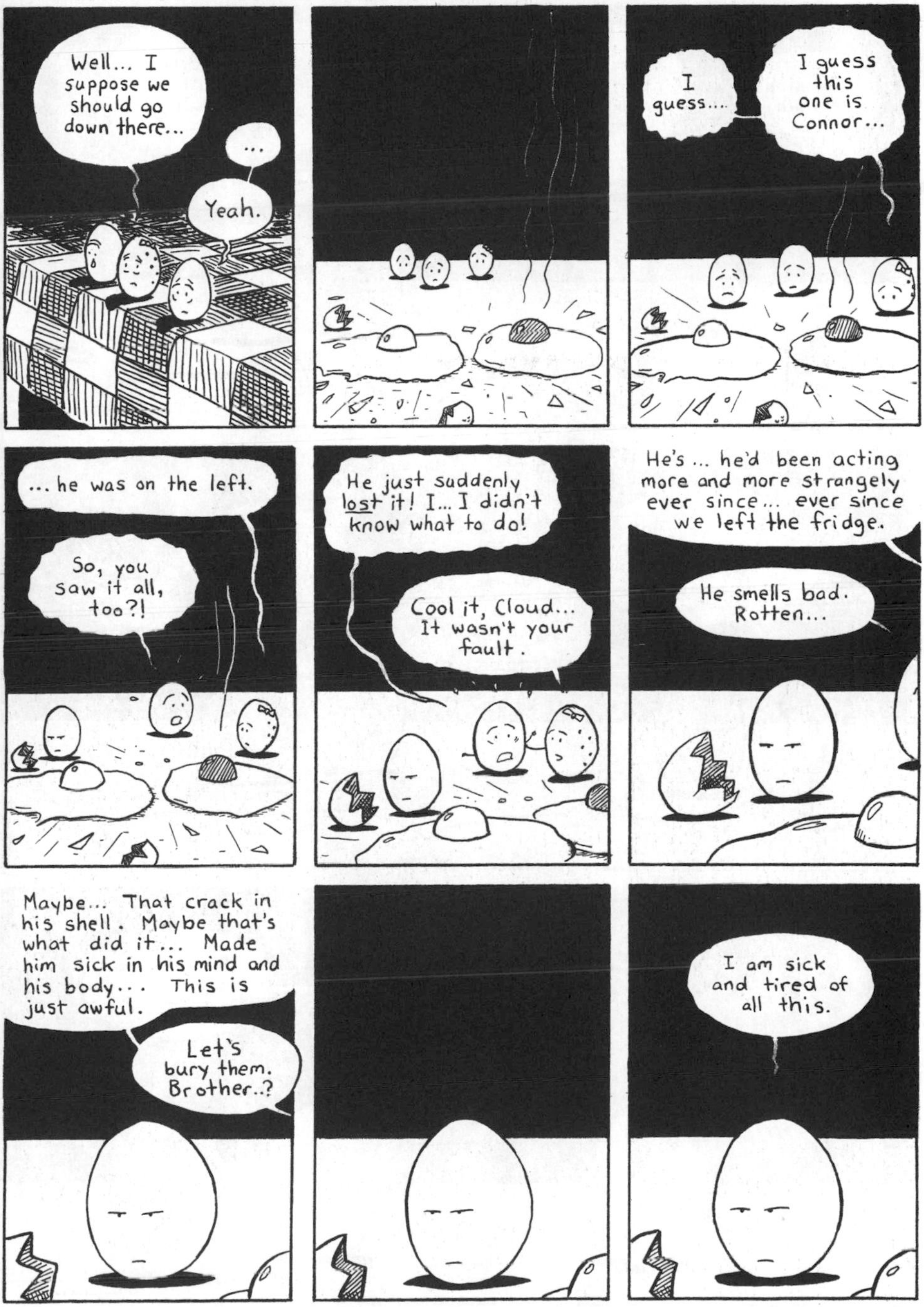
Well... I suppose we should go down there...
...
Yeah.
I guess....
I guess this one is Connor...
... he was on the left.
So, you saw it all, too?!
He just suddenly lost it! I... I didn't know what to do!
Cool it, Cloud... It wasn't your fault.
He's ... he'd been acting more and more strangely ever since... ever since we left the fridge.
He smells bad. Rotten...
Maybe... That crack in his shell. Maybe that's what did it... Made him sick in his mind and his body... This is just awful.
Let's bury them. Brother..?
I am sick and tired of all this.

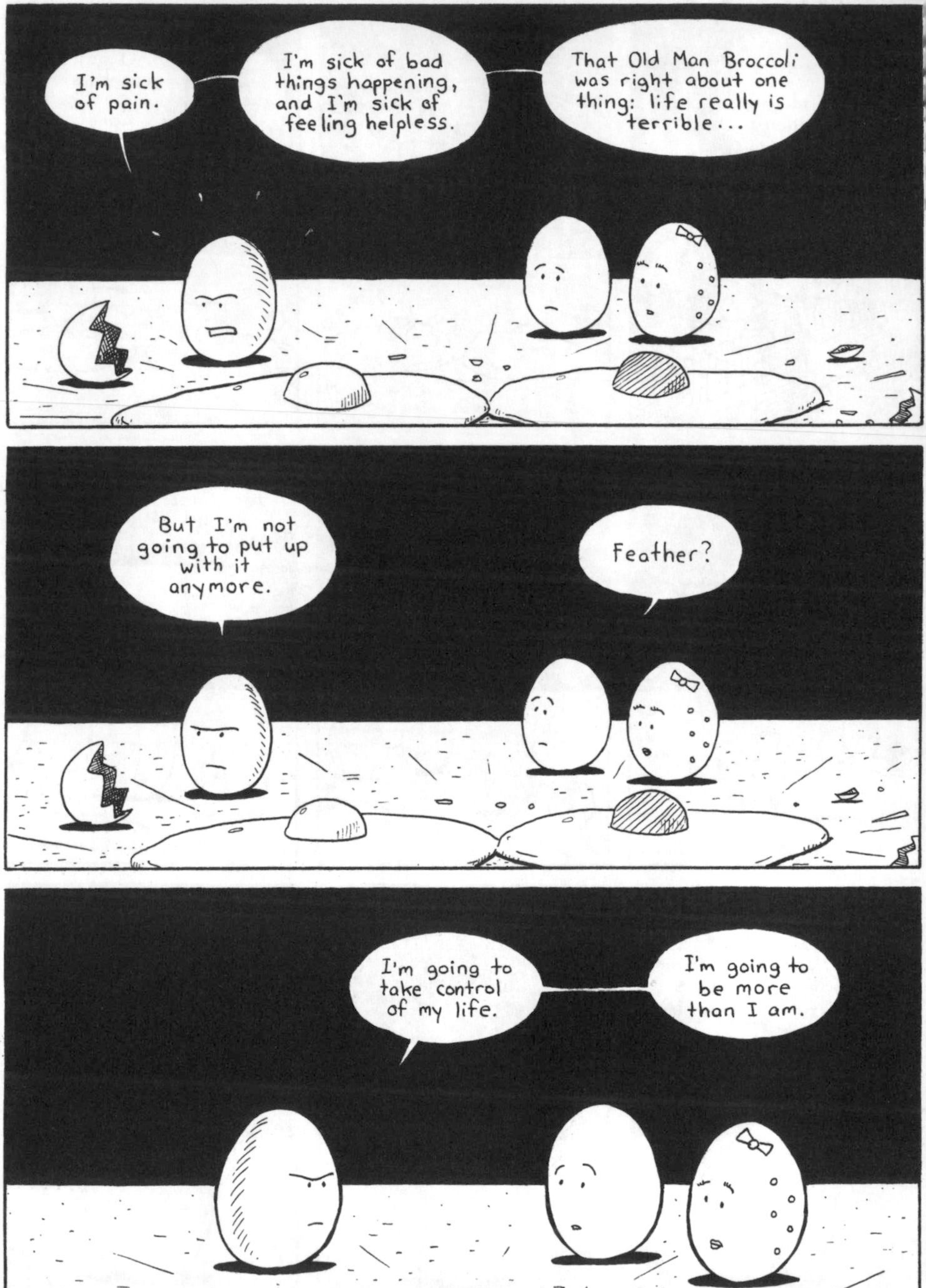
I'm sick of pain.
I'm sick of bad things happening, and I'm sick of feeling helpless.
That Old Man Broccoli was right about one thing: life really is terrible...
But I'm not going to put up with it anymore.
Feather?
I'm going to take control of my life.
I'm going to be more than I am.

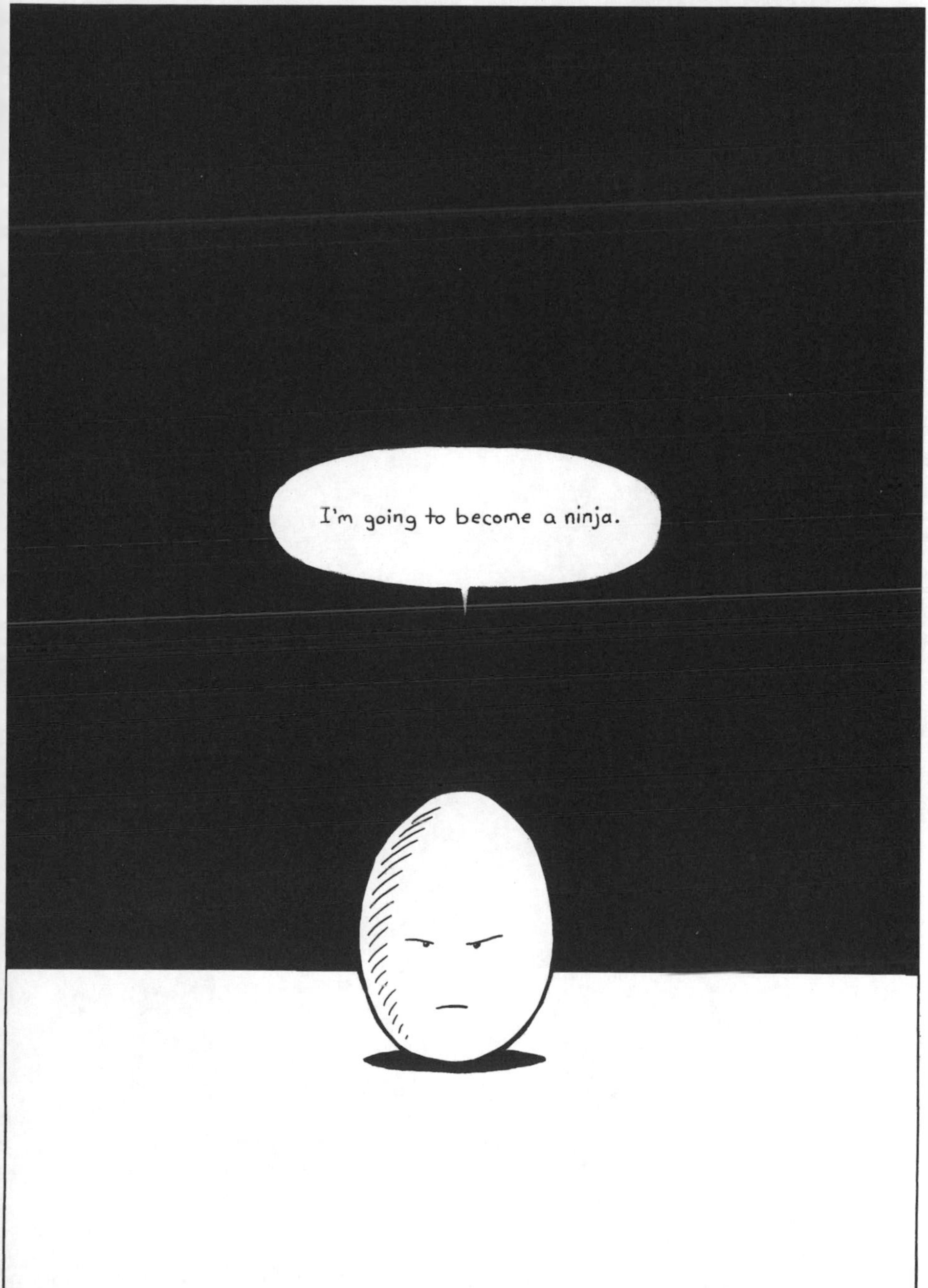
I'm going to become a ninja.

End of Act 2...

3

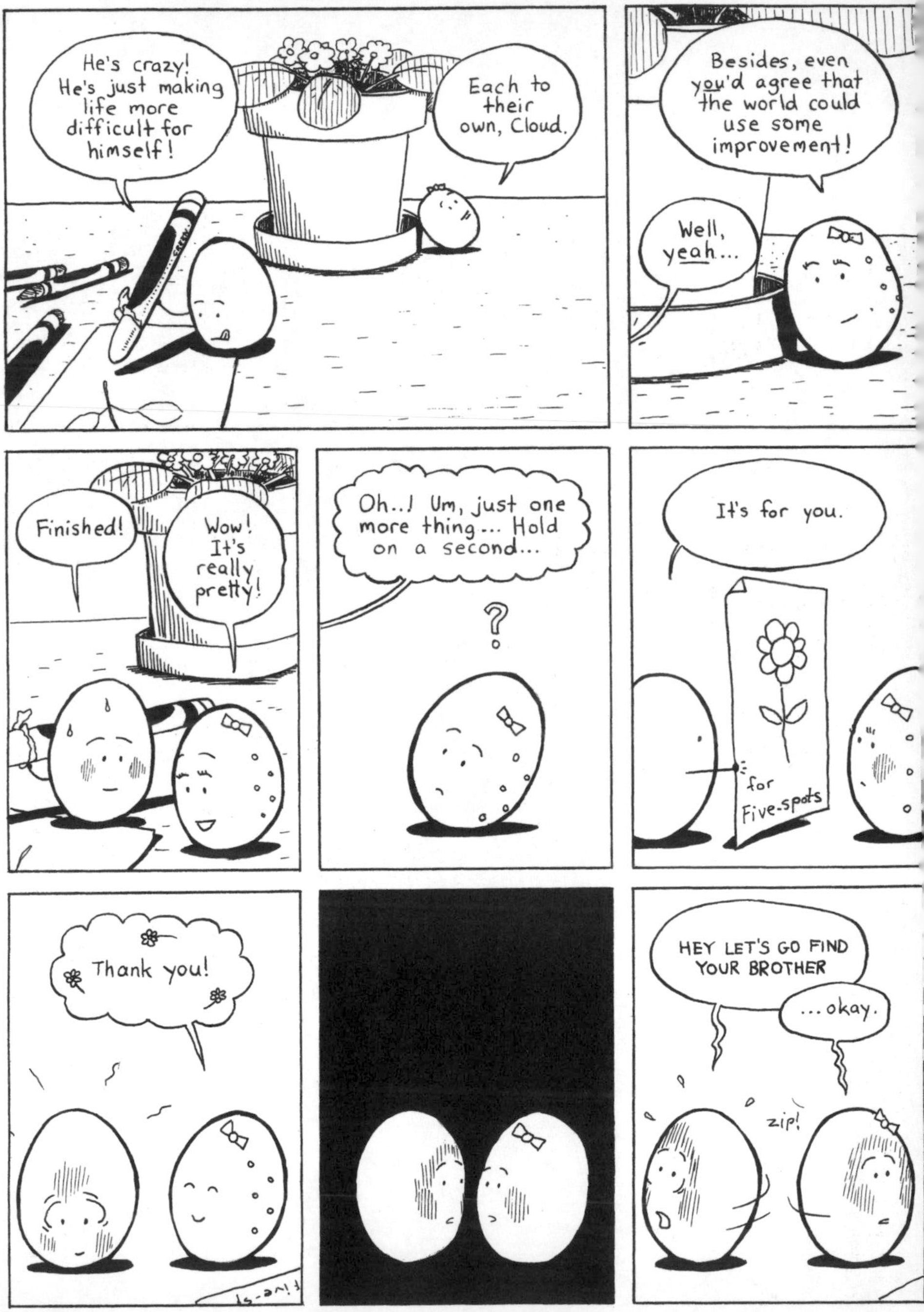
He's crazy! He's just making life more difficult for himself!
Each to their own, Cloud.
Besides, even you'd agree that the world could use some improvement!
Well, yeah...
Finished!
Wow! It's really pretty!
Oh..! Um, just one more thing... Hold on a second...
?
It's for you.
for Five-spots
Thank you!
HEY LET'S GO FIND YOUR BROTHER
...okay.
zip!

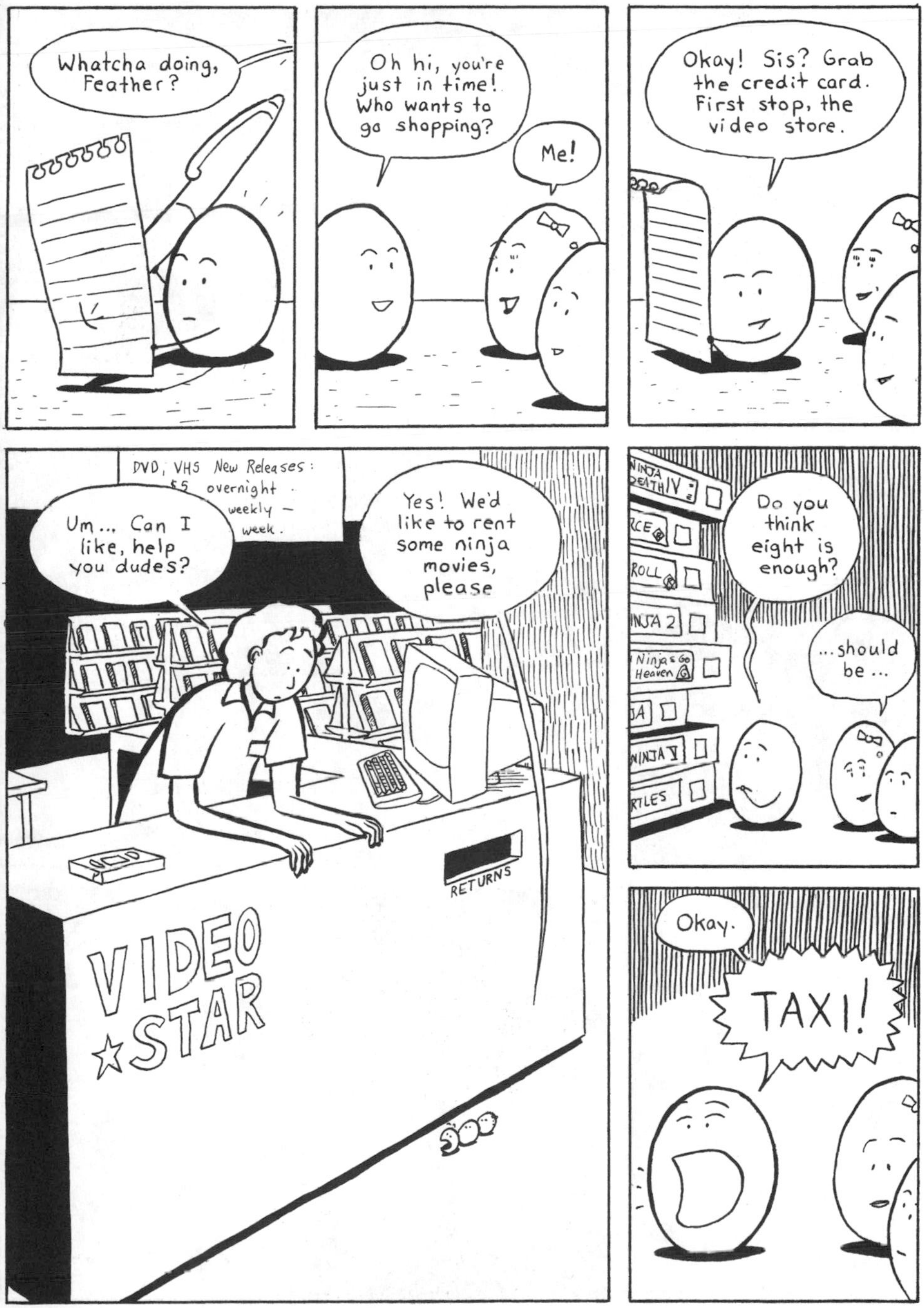
Whatcha doing, Feather?
Oh hi, you're just in time! Who wants to go shopping?
Me!
Okay! Sis? Grab the credit card. First stop, the video store.
DVD, VHS New Releases:
$5 overnight
weekly —
week.
Um... Can I like, help you dudes?
Yes! We'd like to rent some ninja movies, please
RETURNS
VIDEO ☆STAR
NINJA DEATH IV
RCE
ROLL
NINJA 2
Ninjas Go Heaven
JA
NINJA V
RTLES
Do you think eight is enough?
...should be...
Okay.
TAXI!

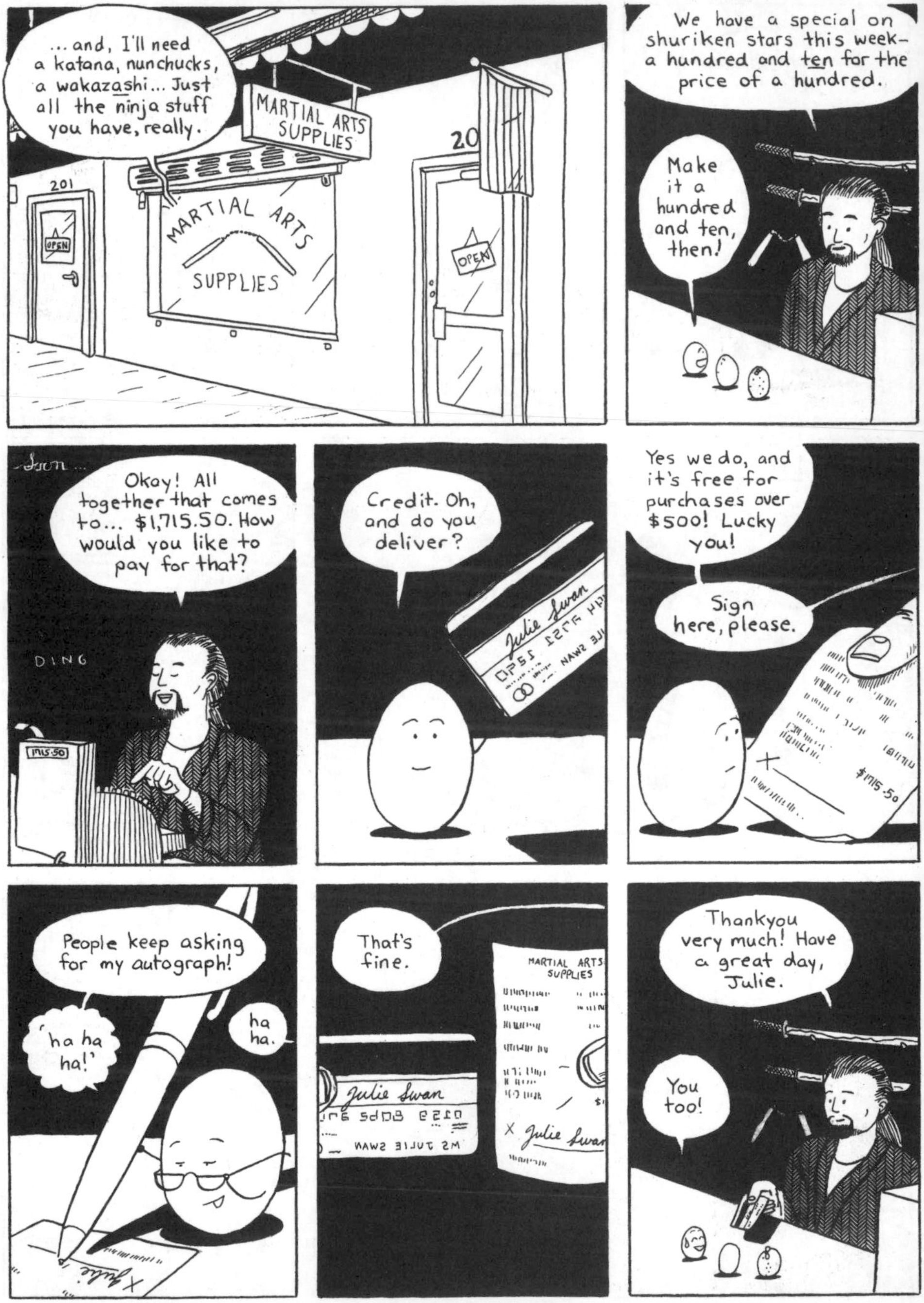
... and, I'll need a katana, nunchucks, a wakazashi... Just all the ninja stuff you have, really.
MARTIAL ARTS SUPPLIES
201
OPEN
MARTIAL ARTS SUPPLIES
20
OPEN
We have a special on shuriken stars this week- a hundred and ten for the price of a hundred.
Make it a hundred and ten, then!
Okay! All together that comes to... $1,715.50. How would you like to pay for that?
DING
1715.50
Credit. Oh, and do you deliver?
Julie Swan
Yes we do, and it's free for purchases over $500! Lucky you!
Sign here, please.
$1715.50
People keep asking for my autograph!
'ha ha ha!'
ha ha.
Julie
That's fine.
Julie Swan
MS JULIE SWAN
MARTIAL ARTS SUPPLIES
Julie Swan
Thankyou very much! Have a great day, Julie.
You too!

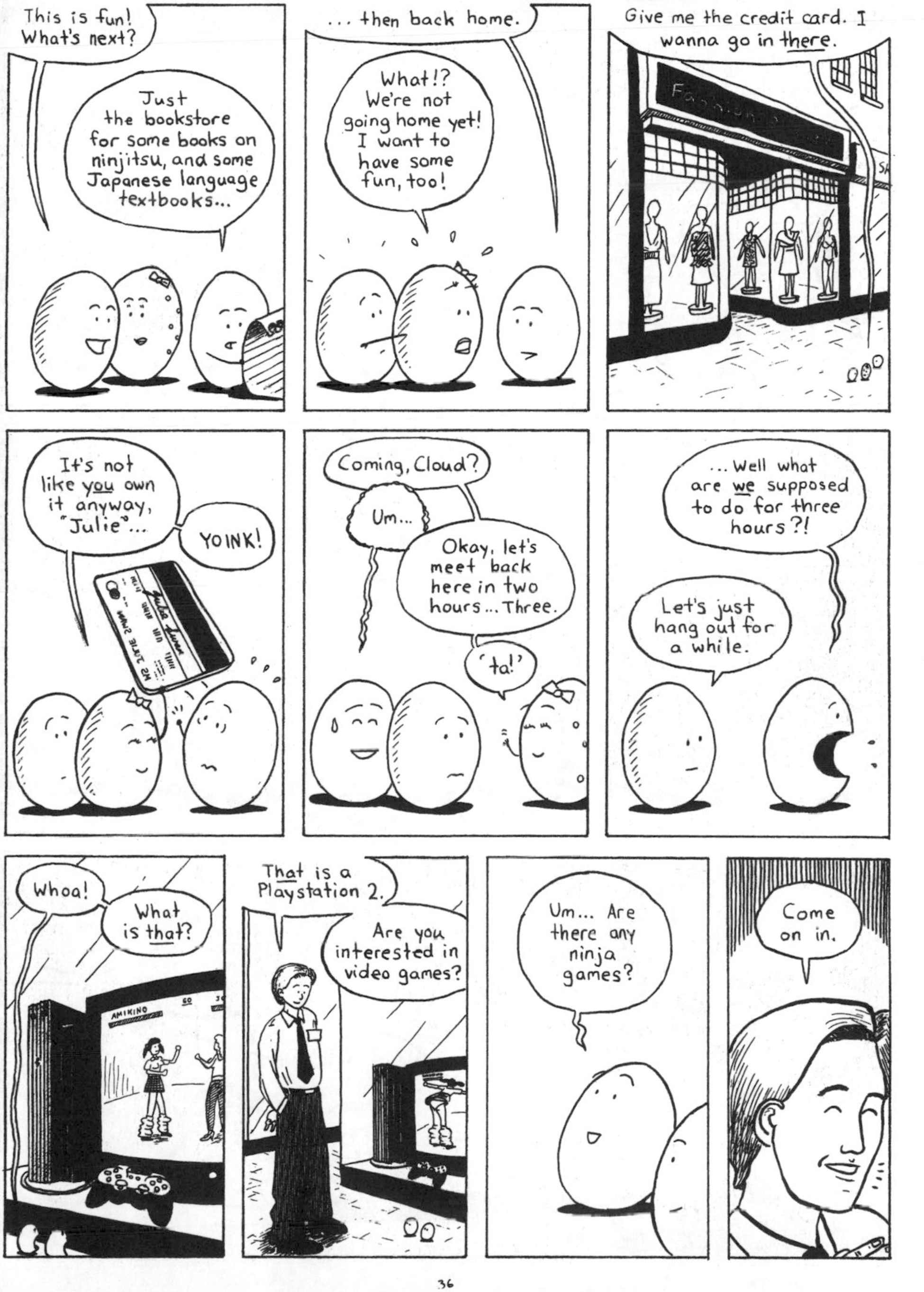
This is fun! What's next?
Just the bookstore for some books on ninjitsu, and some Japanese language textbooks...
... then back home.
What!? We're not going home yet! I want to have some fun, too!
Give me the credit card. I wanna go in there.
It's not like you own it anyway, "Julie"...
YOINK!
Coming, Cloud?
Um...
Okay, let's meet back here in two hours... Three.
'ta!'
...Well what are we supposed to do for three hours?!
Let's just hang out for a while.
Whoa!
What is that?
That is a Playstation 2.
Are you interested in video games?
Um... Are there any ninja games?
Come on in.

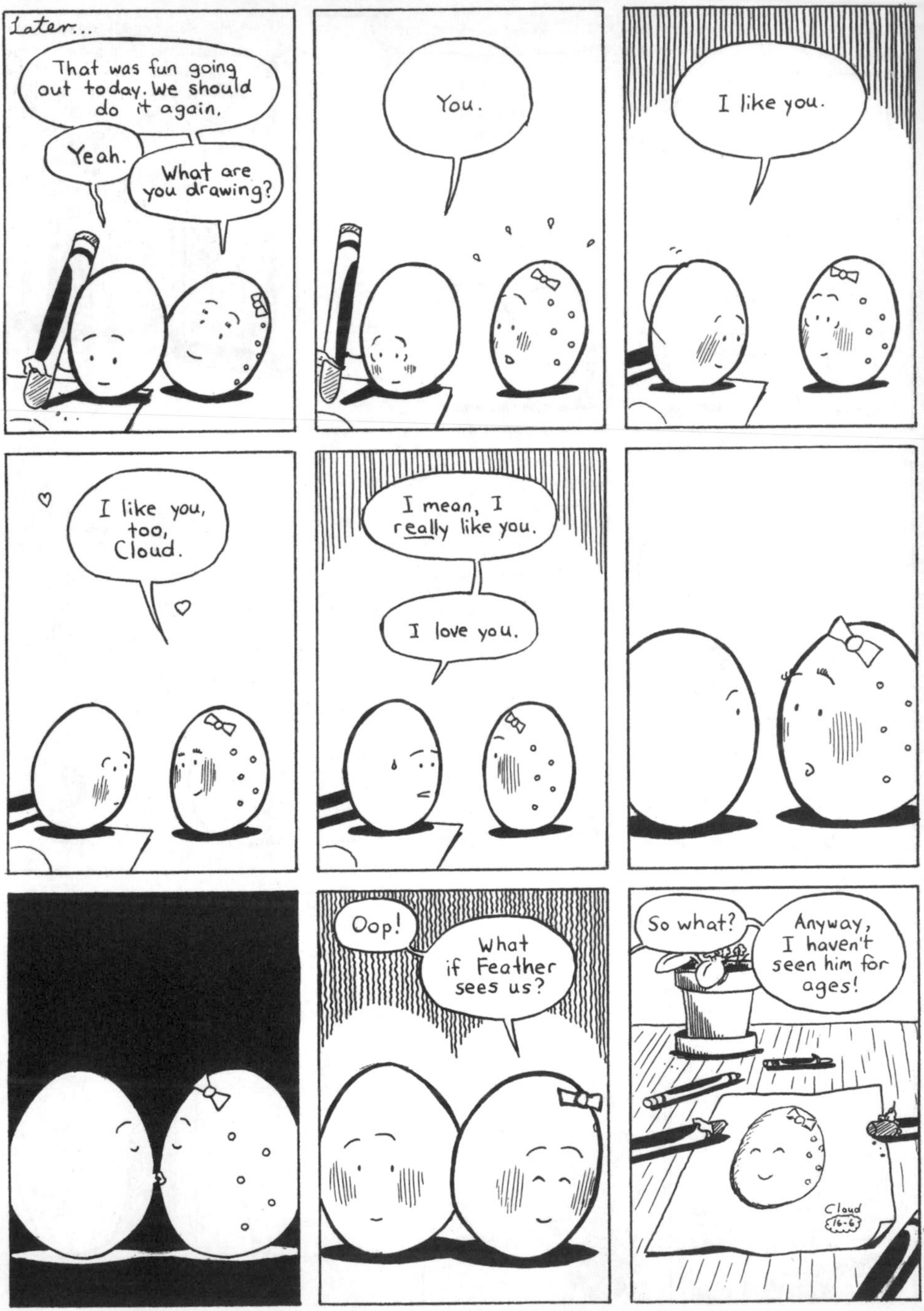
Later...
That was fun going out today. We should do it again.
Yeah.
What are you drawing?
You.
I like you.
I like you, too, Cloud.
I mean, I really like you.
I love you.
Oop!
What if Feather sees us?
So what?
Anyway, I haven't seen him for ages!
Cloud 16-6

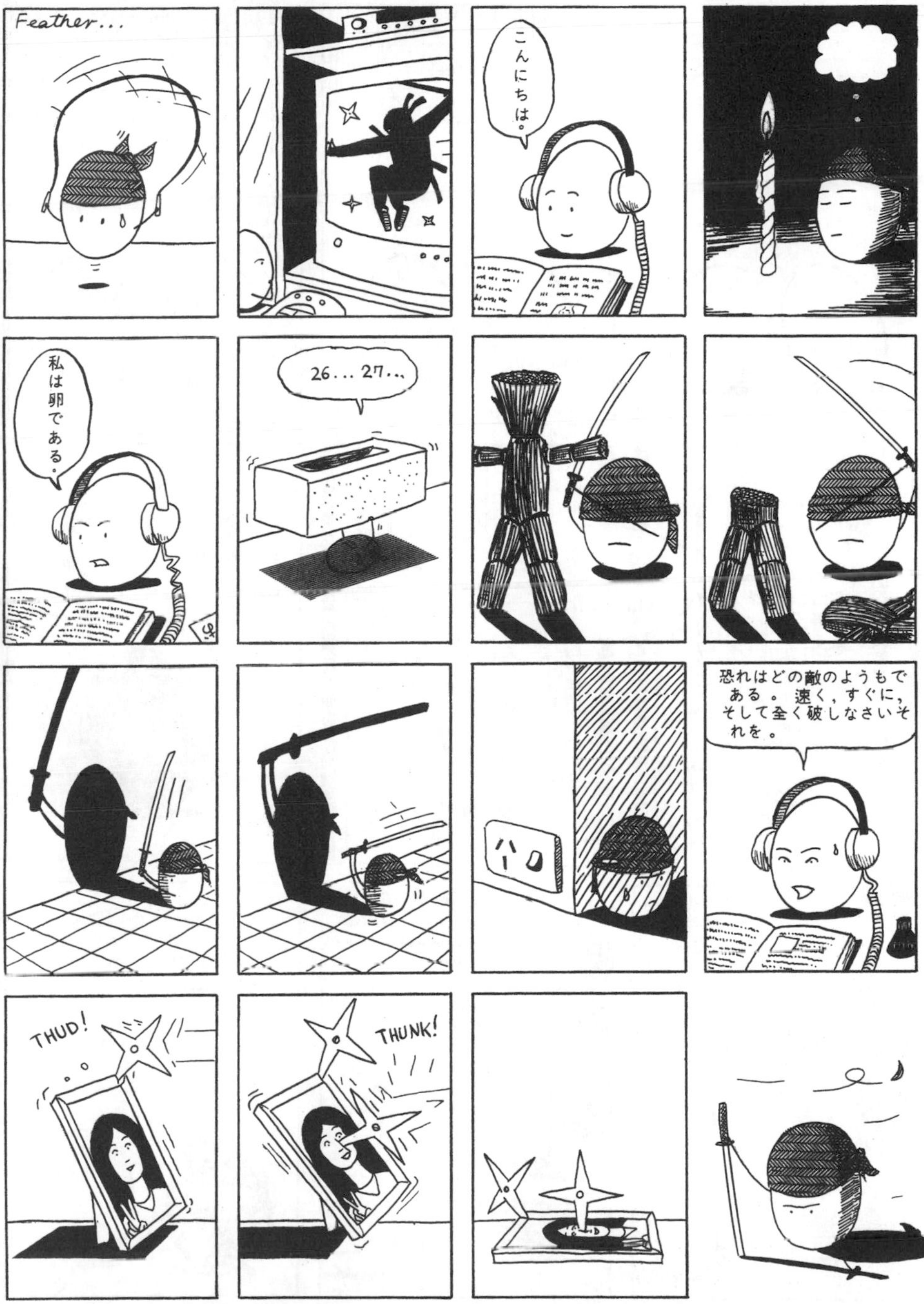
Feather...
こんにちは。
私は卵である。
26... 27...
恐れはどの敵のようもである。速く，すぐに，そして全く破しなさいそれを。
THUD!
THUNK!

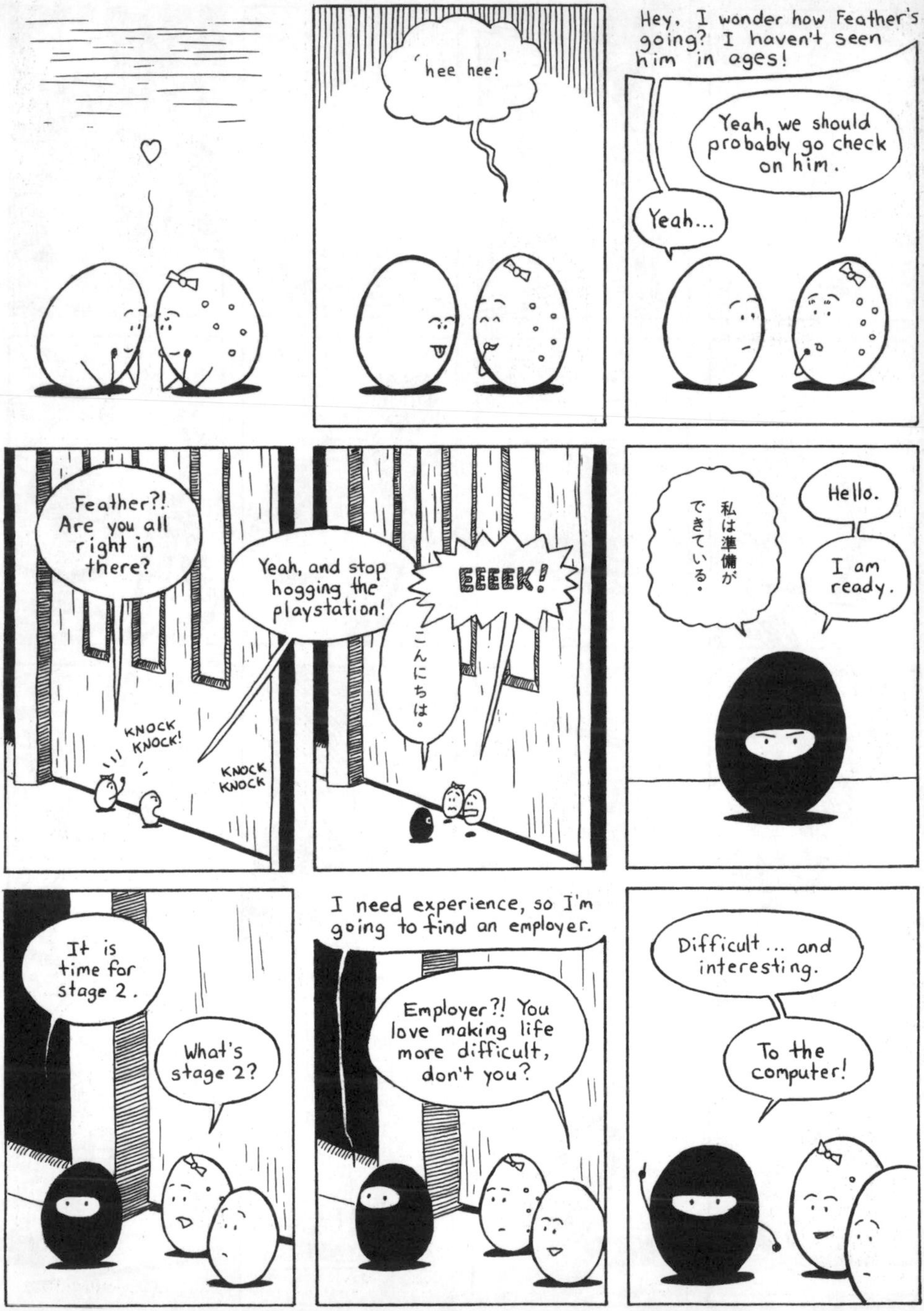

'hee hee!'
Hey, I wonder how Feather's going? I haven't seen him in ages!
Yeah...
Yeah, we should probably go check on him.
Feather?! Are you all right in there?
KNOCK KNOCK!
KNOCK KNOCK
Yeah, and stop hogging the playstation!
EEEEK!
こんにちは。
Hello.
私は準備ができている。
I am ready.
It is time for stage 2.
What's stage 2?
I need experience, so I'm going to find an employer.
Employer?! You love making life more difficult, don't you?
Difficult... and interesting.
To the computer!

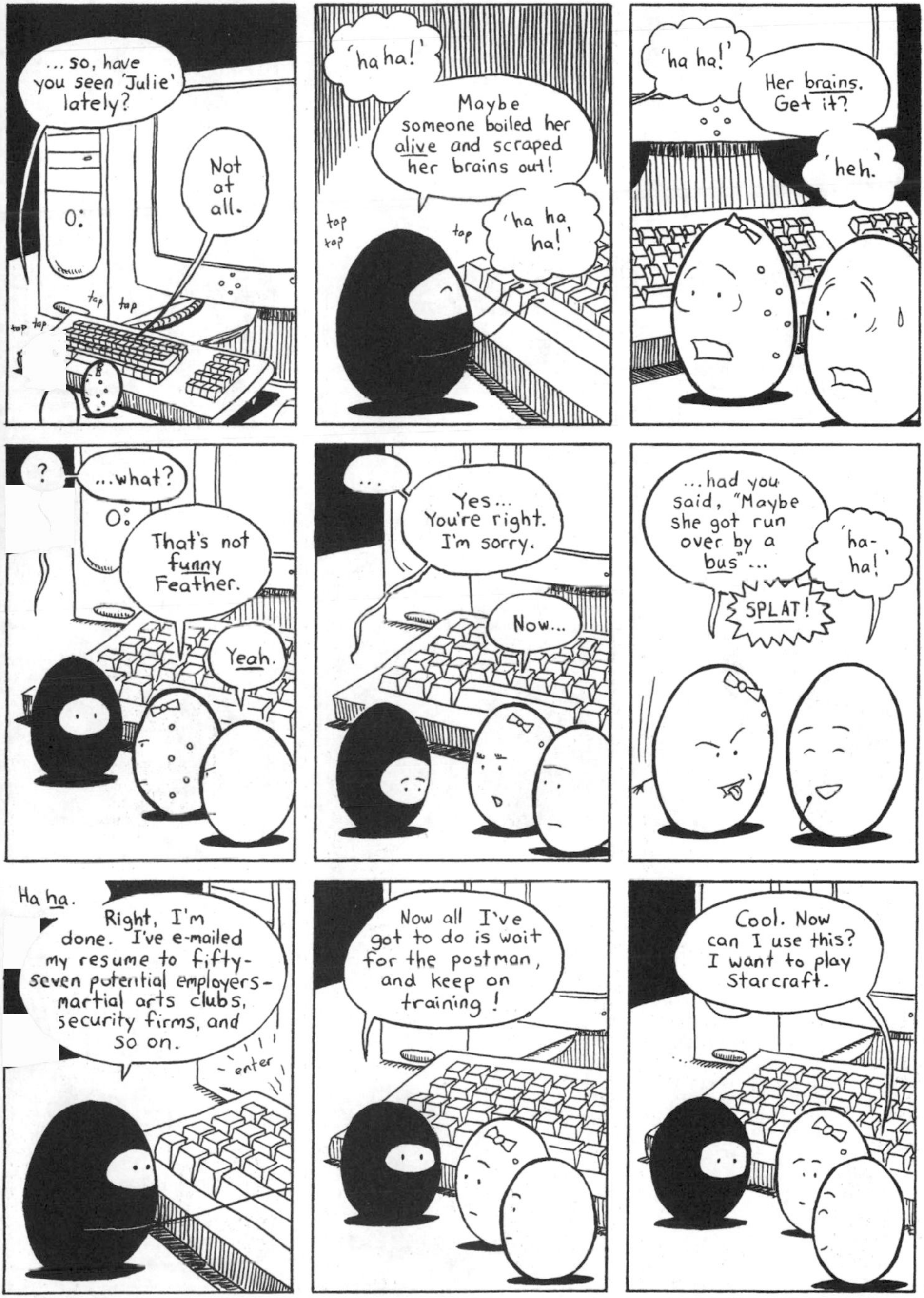
...so, have you seen 'Julie' lately?
Not at all.
tap tap
tap tap
'ha ha!'
Maybe someone boiled her alive and scraped her brains out!
tap tap
tap
'ha ha ha!'
'ha ha!'
Her brains. Get it?
'heh.'
?
...what?
That's not funny Feather.
Yeah.
...
Yes... You're right. I'm sorry.
Now...
...had you said, "Maybe she got run over by a bus"...
SPLAT!
'ha-ha!'
Ha ha.
Right, I'm done. I've e-mailed my resume to fifty-seven potential employers - martial arts clubs, security firms, and so on.
enter
Now all I've got to do is wait for the postman, and keep on training!
Cool. Now can I use this? I want to play Starcraft.

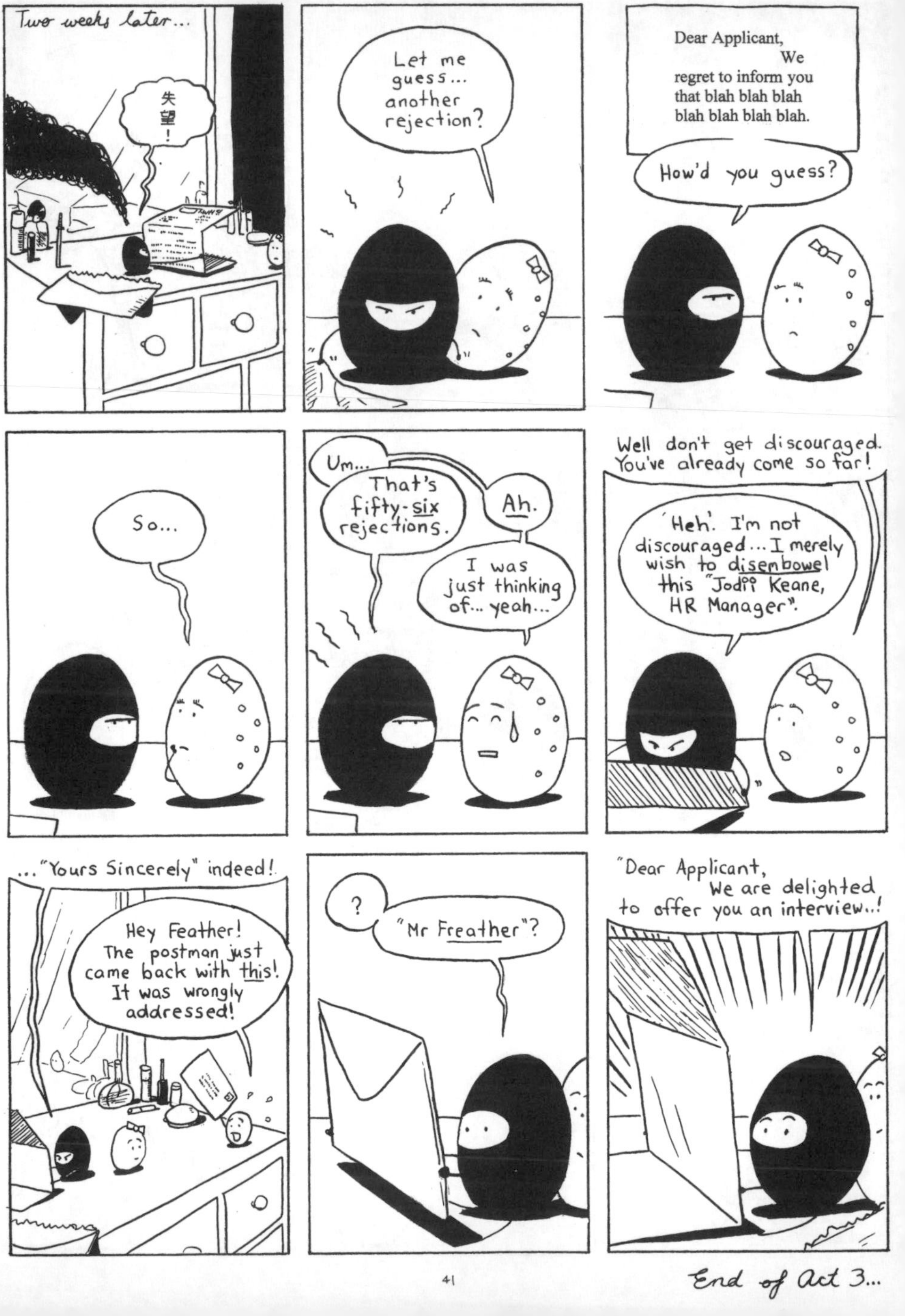
Two weeks later...
失望!
Let me guess... another rejection?
Dear Applicant,
We regret to inform you that blah blah blah blah blah blah blah.
How'd you guess?
So...
Um...
That's fifty-six rejections.
Ah.
I was just thinking of... yeah...
Well don't get discouraged. You've already come so far!
'Heh'. I'm not discouraged... I merely wish to disembowel this "Jodii Keane, HR Manager".
..."Yours Sincerely" indeed!
Hey Feather! The postman just came back with this! It was wrongly addressed!
?
"Mr Freather"?
"Dear Applicant,
We are delighted to offer you an interview..!

End of Act 3...

4

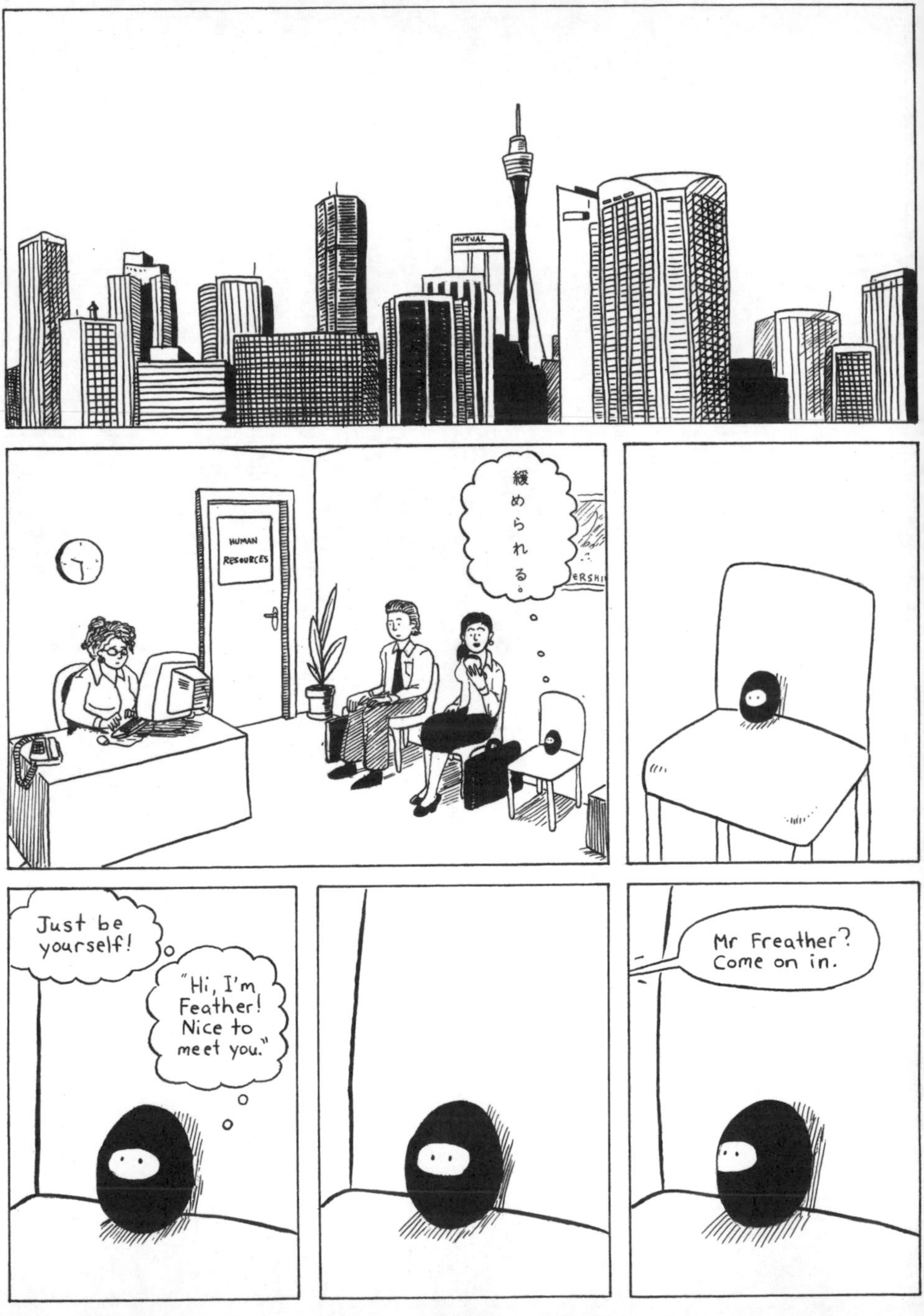
MUTUAL
HUMAN RESOURCES
緩められる。
Just be yourself!
"Hi, I'm Feather! Nice to meet you."
Mr Freather? Come on in.

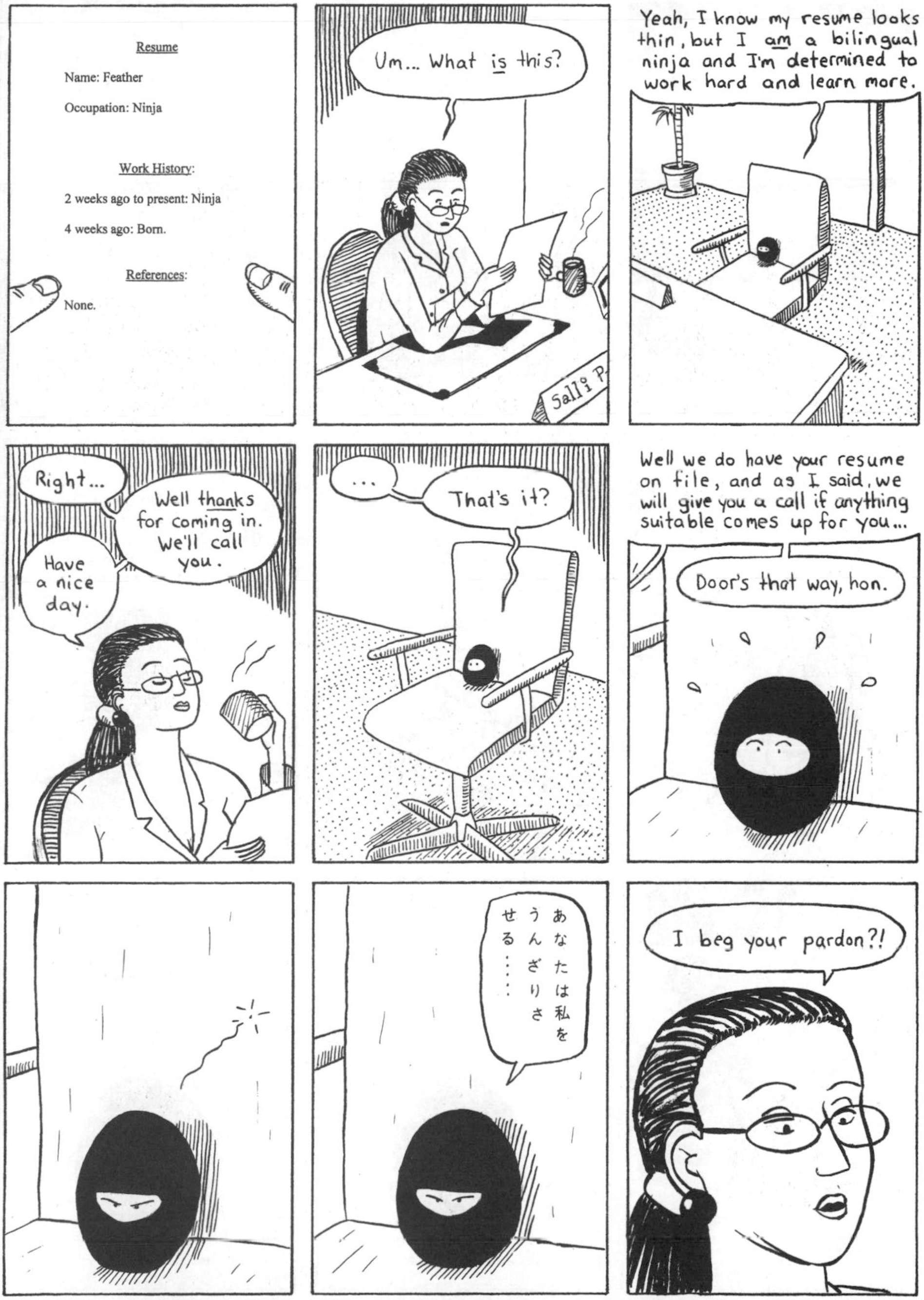
Resume
Name: Feather
Occupation: Ninja
Work History:
2 weeks ago to present: Ninja
4 weeks ago: Born.
References:
None.
Um... What is this?
Salli P.
Yeah, I know my resume looks thin, but I am a bilingual ninja and I'm determined to work hard and learn more.
Right...
Well thanks for coming in. We'll call you.
Have a nice day.
...
That's it?
Well we do have your resume on file, and as I said, we will give you a call if anything suitable comes up for you...
Door's that way, hon.
あなたは私をうんざりさせる・・・・
I beg your pardon?!

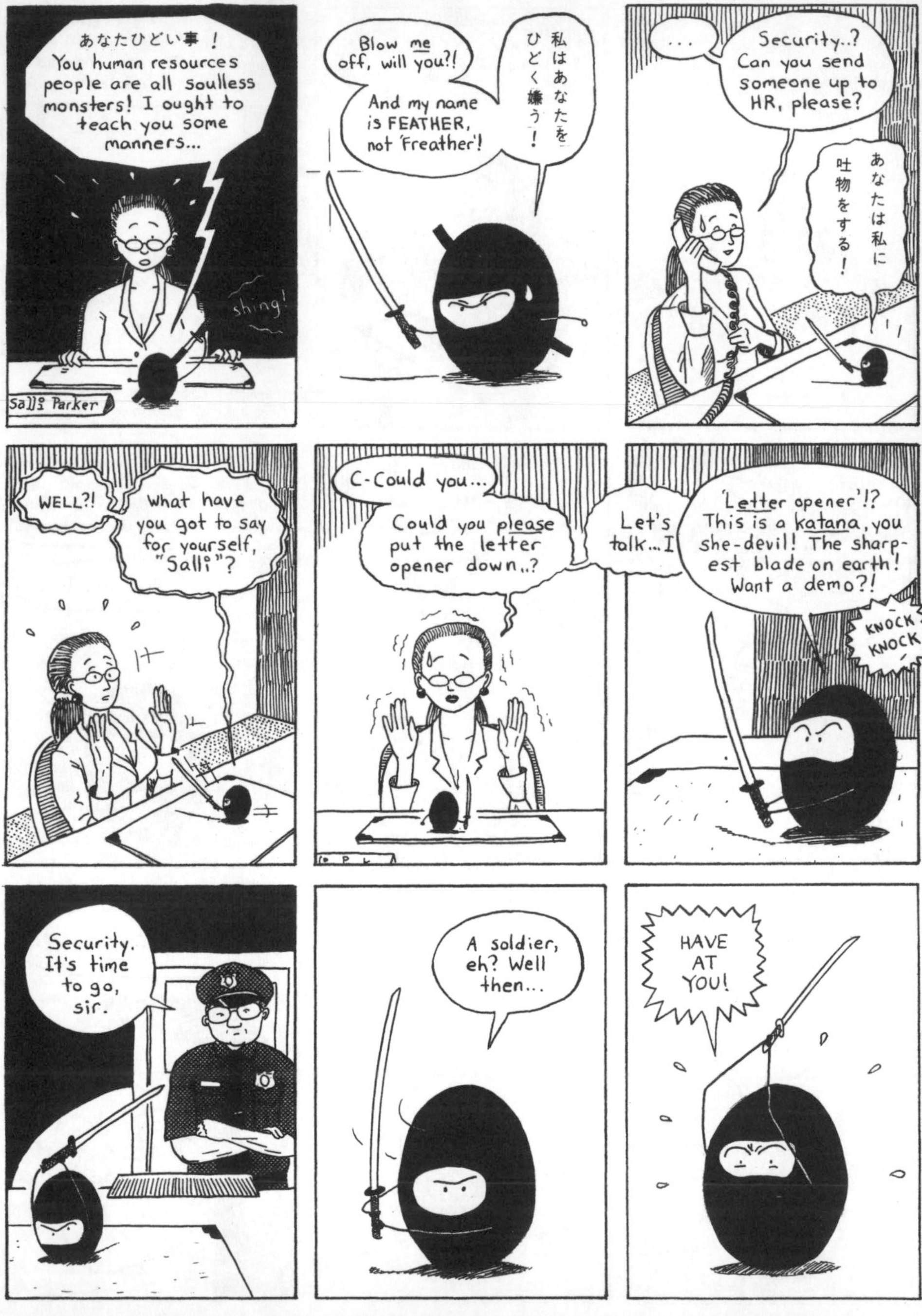

あなたひどい事！
You human resources people are all soulless monsters! I ought to teach you some manners...
shing!
Salli Parker
Blow me off, will you?!
And my name is FEATHER, not 'Freather'!
私はあなたをひどく嫌う！
...
Security..? Can you send someone up to HR, please?
あなたは私に吐物をする！
WELL?!
What have you got to say for yourself, "Salli"?
C-Could you...
Could you please put the letter opener down..?
Let's talk... I
'Letter opener'!? This is a katana, you she-devil! The sharpest blade on earth! Want a demo?!
KNOCK KNOCK
Security. It's time to go, sir.
A soldier, eh? Well then...
HAVE AT YOU!

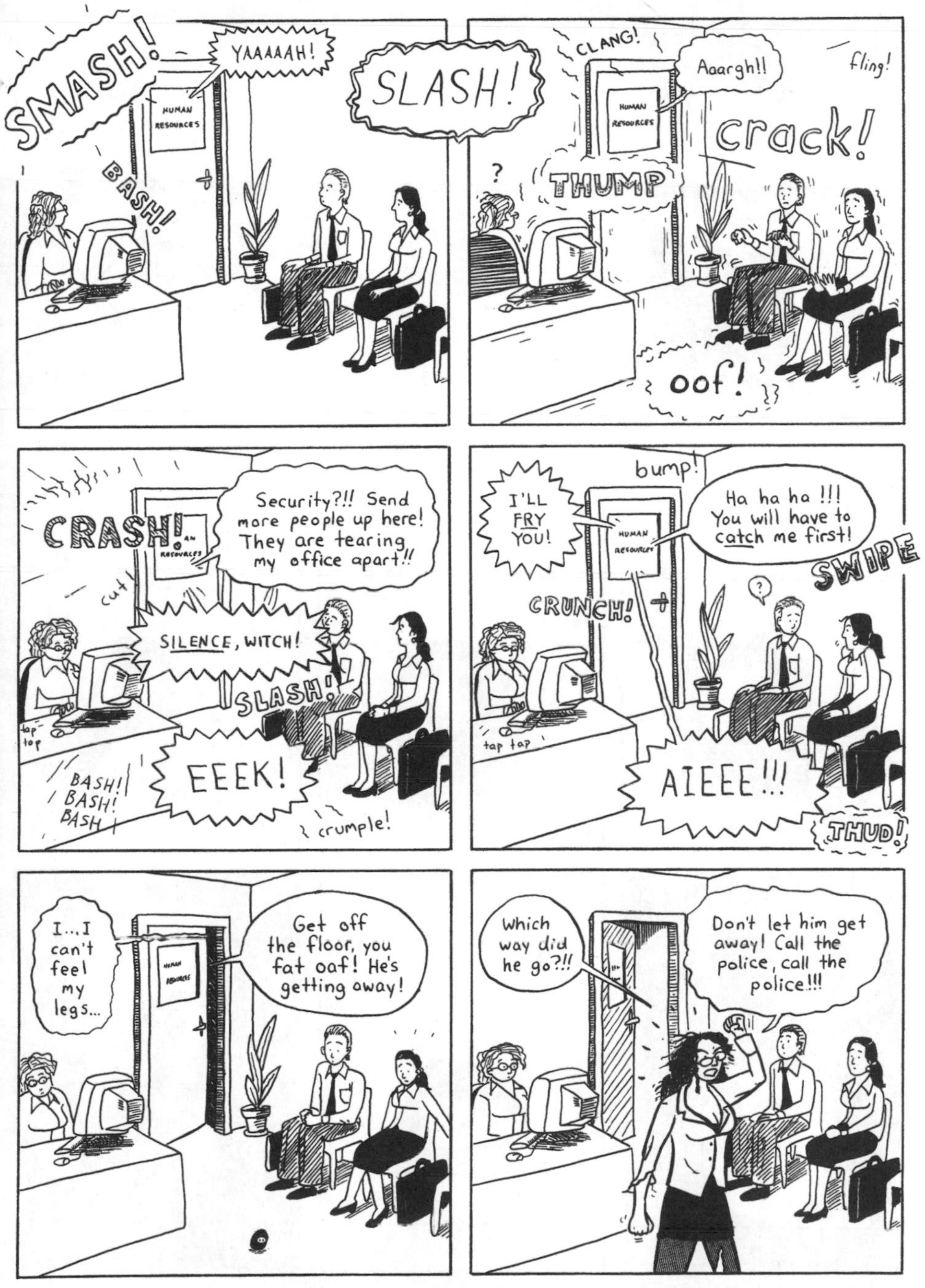
SMASH!
YAAAAAH!
HUMAN RESOURCES
BASH!
SLASH!
CLANG!
Aaargh!!
fling!
HUMAN RESOURCES
crack!
?
THUMP
oof!
CRASH!
Security?!! Send more people up here! They are tearing my office apart!!
cut!
SILENCE, WITCH!
SLASH!
tap tap
EEEK!
BASH! BASH! BASH
crumple!
bump!
I'LL FRY YOU!
HUMAN RESOURCES
Ha ha ha !!! You will have to catch me first!
SWIPE
CRUNCH!
?
tap tap
AIEEE!!!
THUD!
I...I can't feel my legs...
HUMAN RESOURCES
Get off the floor, you fat oaf! He's getting away!
Which way did he go?!!
Don't let him get away! Call the police, call the police!!!

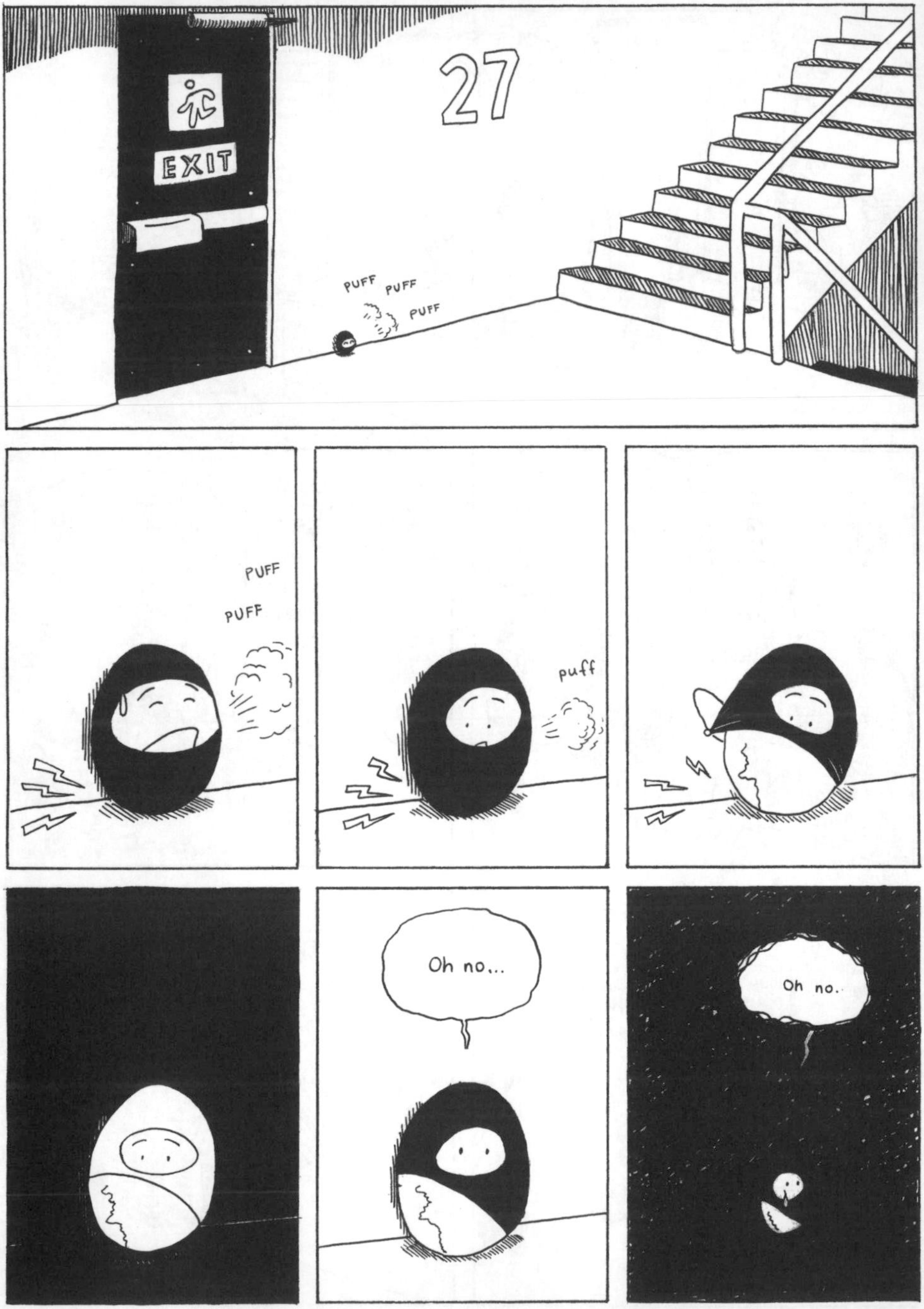
27
EXIT
PUFF
PUFF
PUFF
PUFF
PUFF
puff
Oh no...
Oh no..

End of Act 4...

5

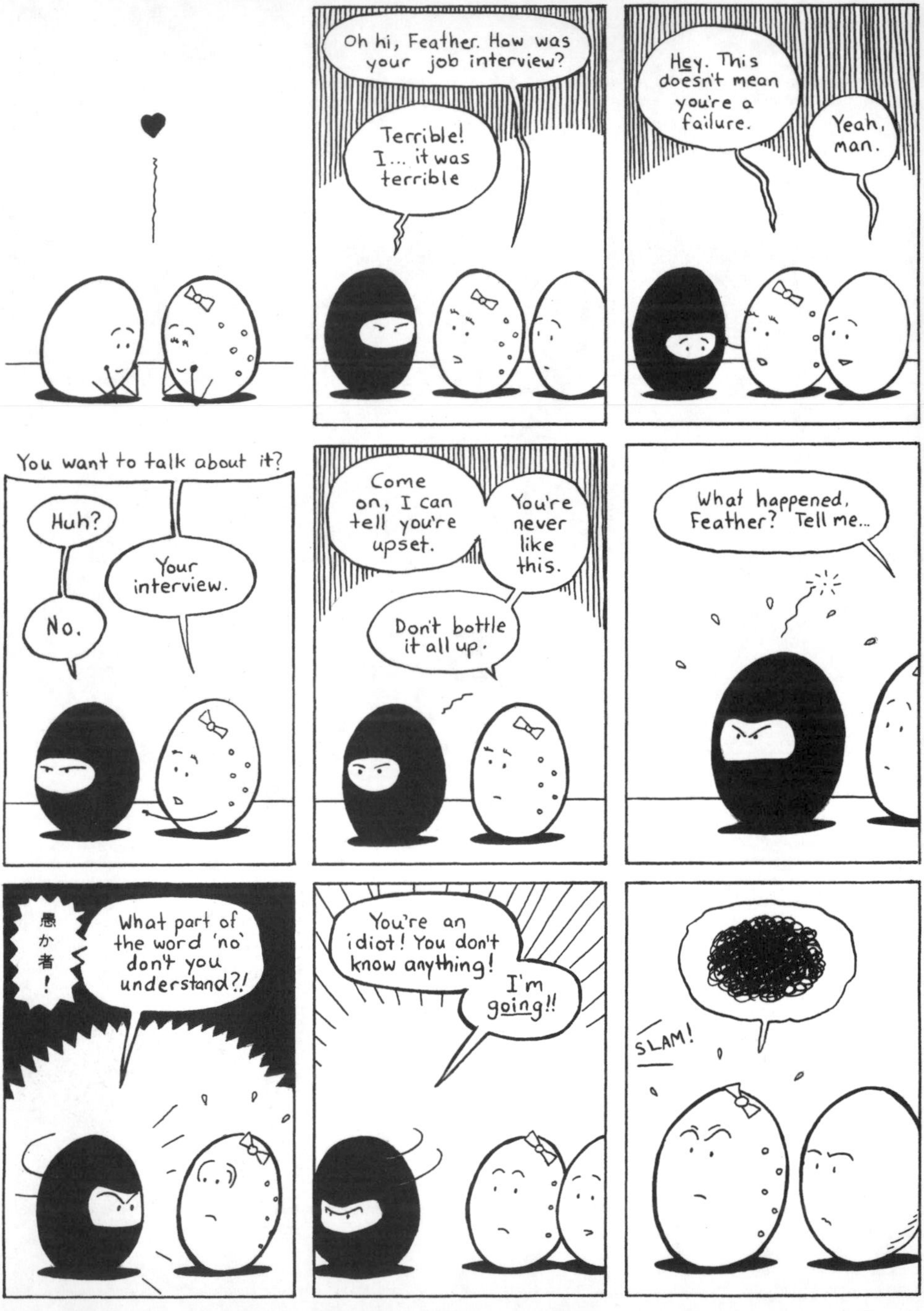
Oh hi, Feather. How was your job interview?
Terrible! I... it was terrible
Hey. This doesn't mean you're a failure.
Yeah, man.
You want to talk about it?
Huh?
Your interview.
No.
Come on, I can tell you're upset.
You're never like this.
Don't bottle it all up.
What happened, Feather? Tell me...
愚か者!
What part of the word 'no' don't you understand?!
You're an idiot! You don't know anything!
I'm going!!
SLAM!

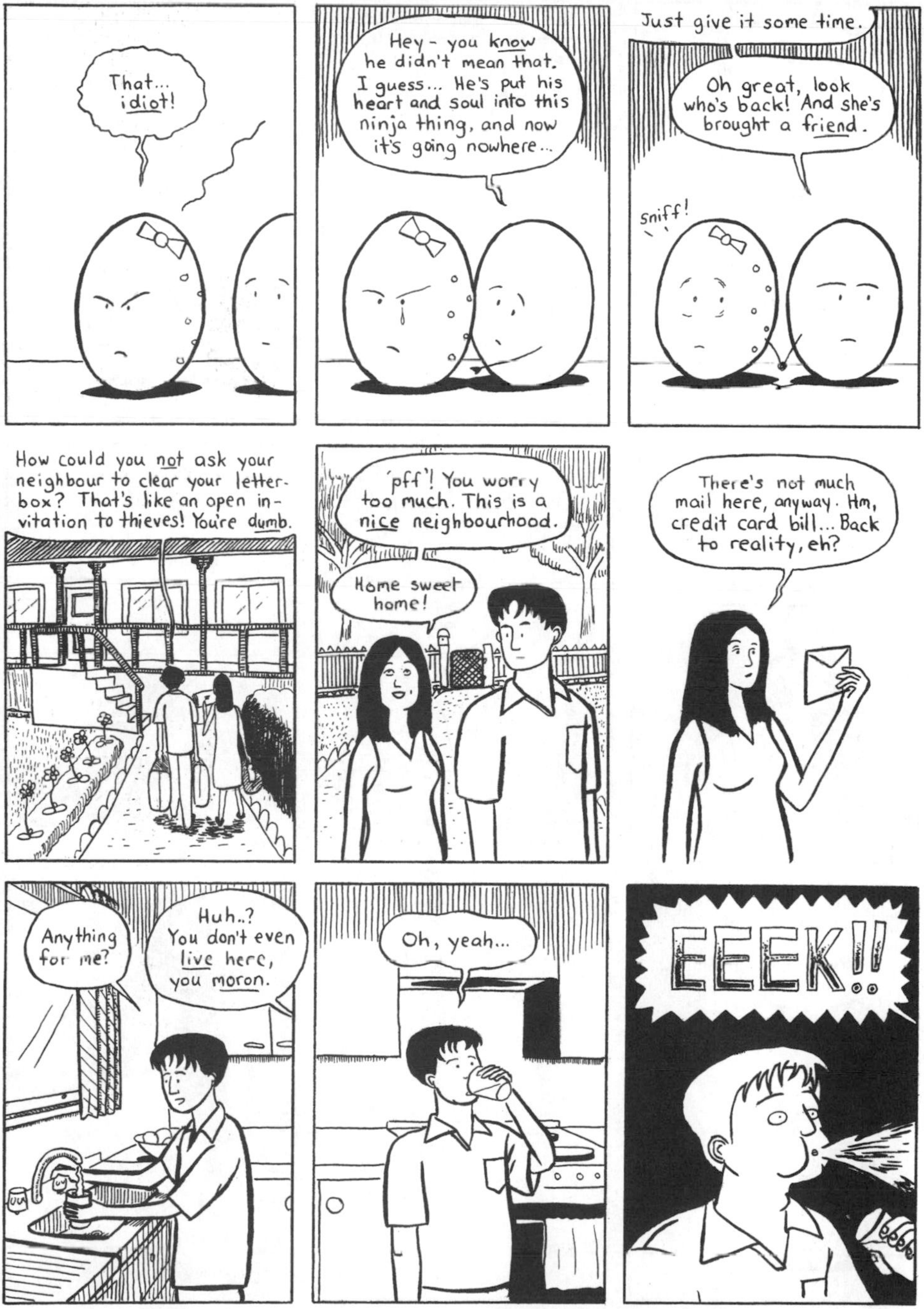

That... idiot!
Hey - you know he didn't mean that. I guess... He's put his heart and soul into this ninja thing, and now it's going nowhere...
Just give it some time.
Oh great, look who's back! And she's brought a friend.
sniff!
How could you not ask your neighbour to clear your letter-box? That's like an open invitation to thieves! You're dumb.
'pff'! You worry too much. This is a nice neighbourhood.
Home sweet home!
There's not much mail here, anyway. Hm, credit card bill... Back to reality, eh?
Anything for me?
Huh..? You don't even live here, you moron.
Oh, yeah...
EEEK!!

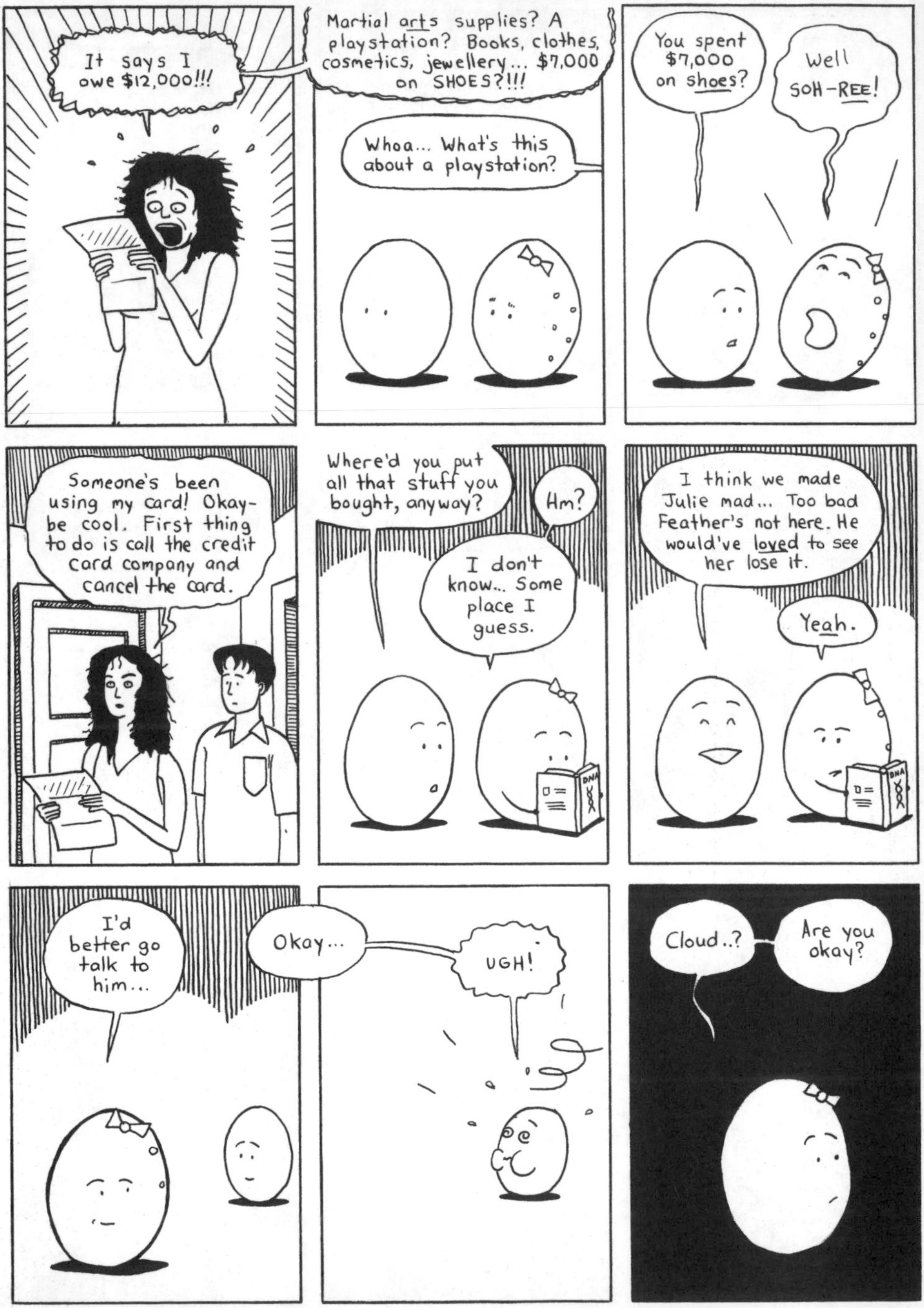
It says I owe $12,000!!!
Martial arts supplies? A playstation? Books, clothes, cosmetics, jewellery... $7,000 on SHOES?!!!
Whoa... What's this about a playstation?
You spent $7,000 on shoes?
Well SOH-REE!
Someone's been using my card! Okay- be cool. First thing to do is call the credit card company and cancel the card.
Where'd you put all that stuff you bought, anyway?
Hm?
I don't know... Some place I guess.
DNA
I think we made Julie mad... Too bad Feather's not here. He would've loved to see her lose it.
Yeah.
DNA
I'd better go talk to him...
Okay...
UGH!
Cloud..?
Are you okay?

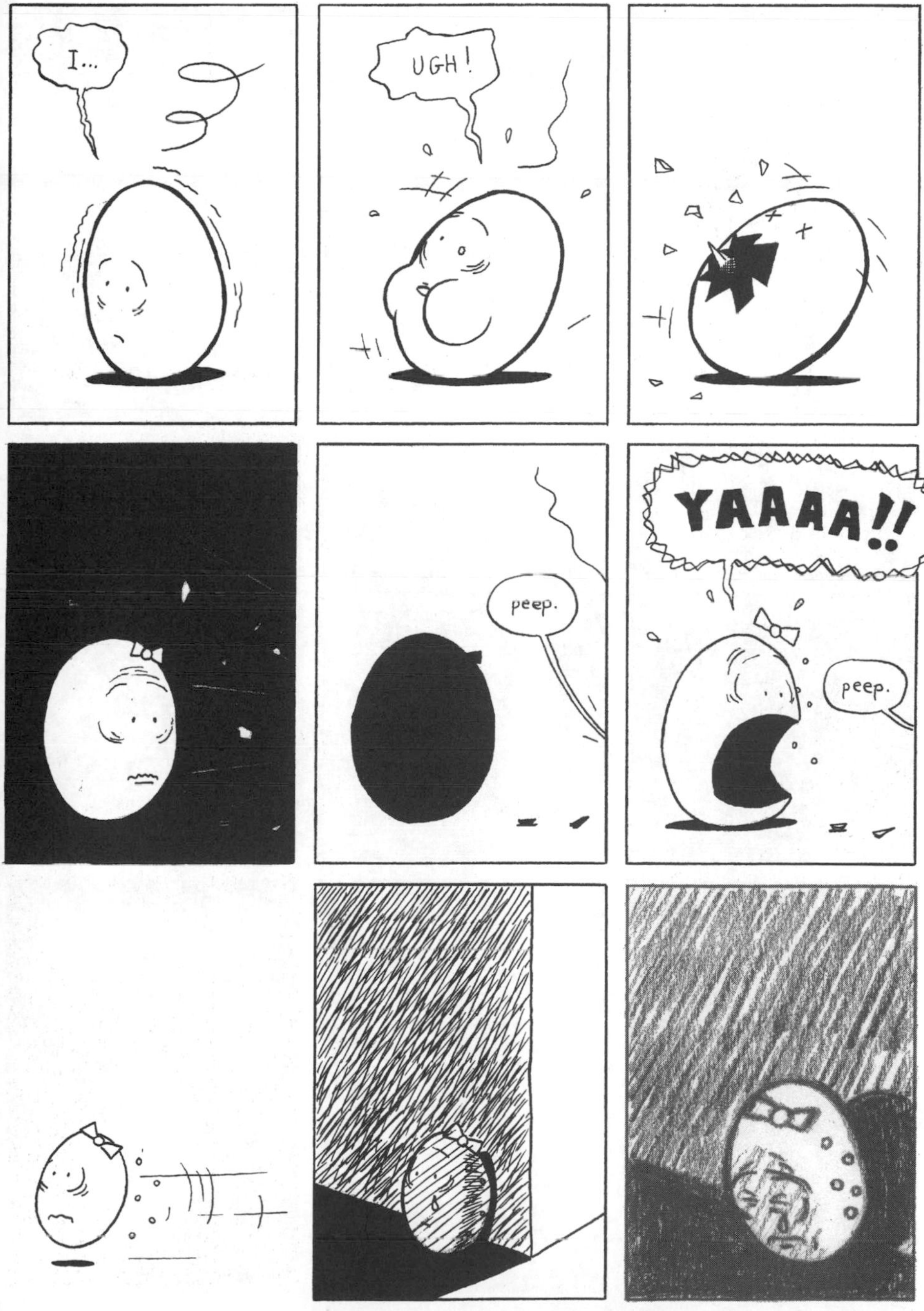
I...
UGH!
peep.
YAAAA!!
peep.

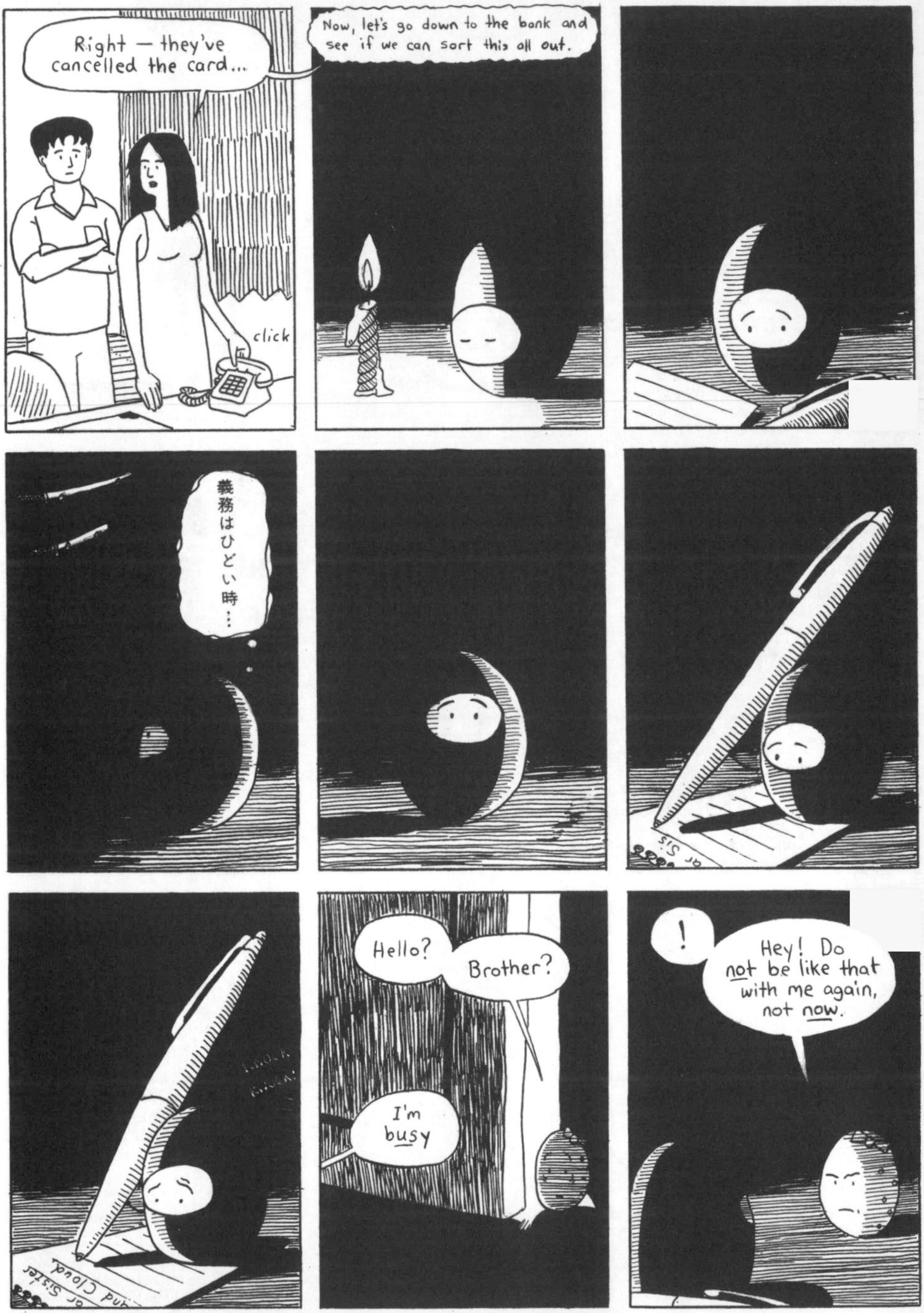
Right — they've cancelled the card...
click
Now, let's go down to the bank and see if we can sort this all out.
義務はひどい時…
Hello?
Brother?
I'm busy
!
Hey! Do not be like that with me again, not now.

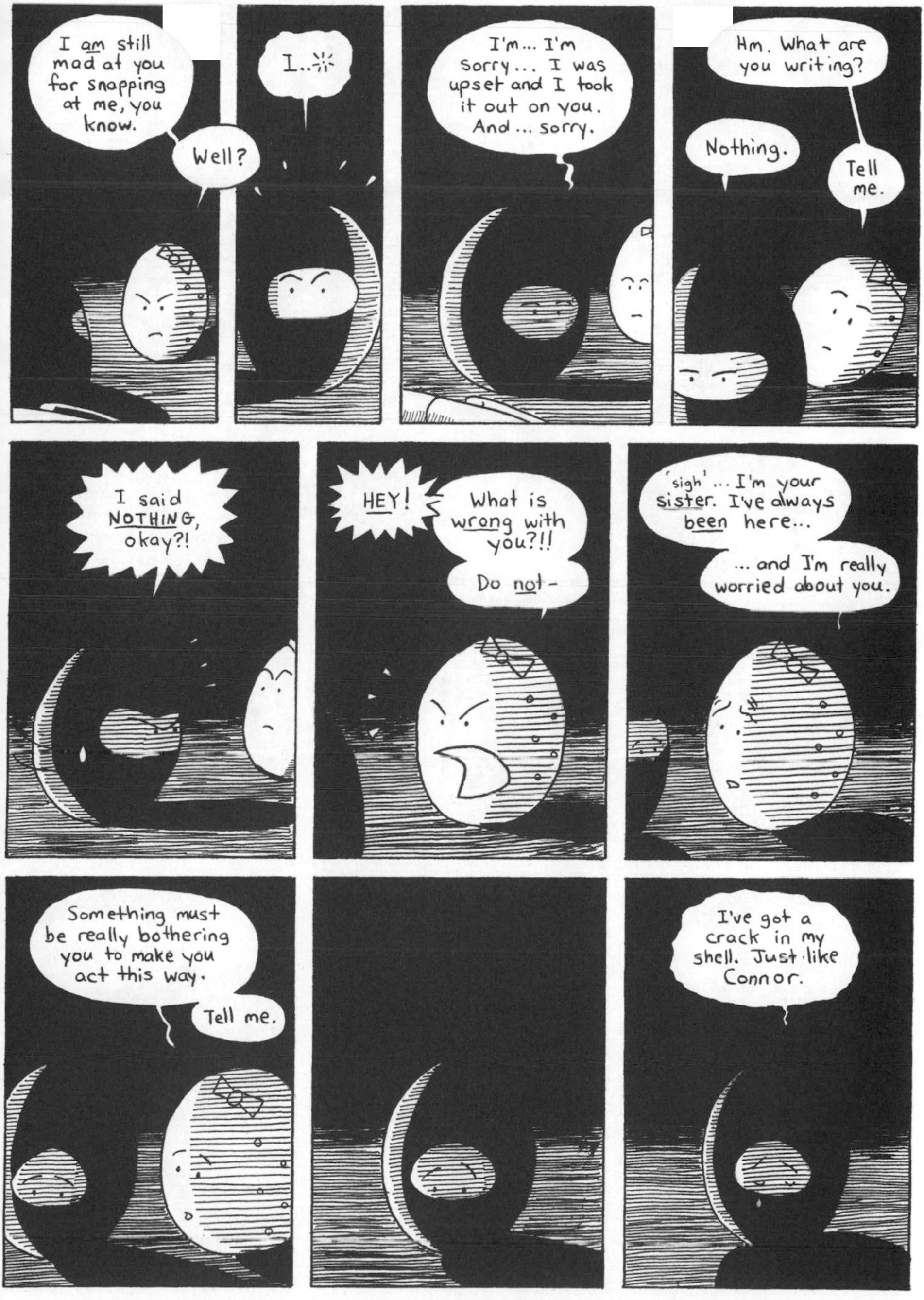
I am still mad at you for snapping at me, you know.
Well?
I..
I'm... I'm sorry... I was upset and I took it out on you. And... sorry.
Hm. What are you writing?
Nothing.
Tell me.
I said NOTHING, okay?!
HEY!
What is wrong with you?!!
Do not-
'sigh'... I'm your sister. I've always been here...
... and I'm really worried about you.
Something must be really bothering you to make you act this way.
Tell me.
I've got a crack in my shell. Just like Connor.

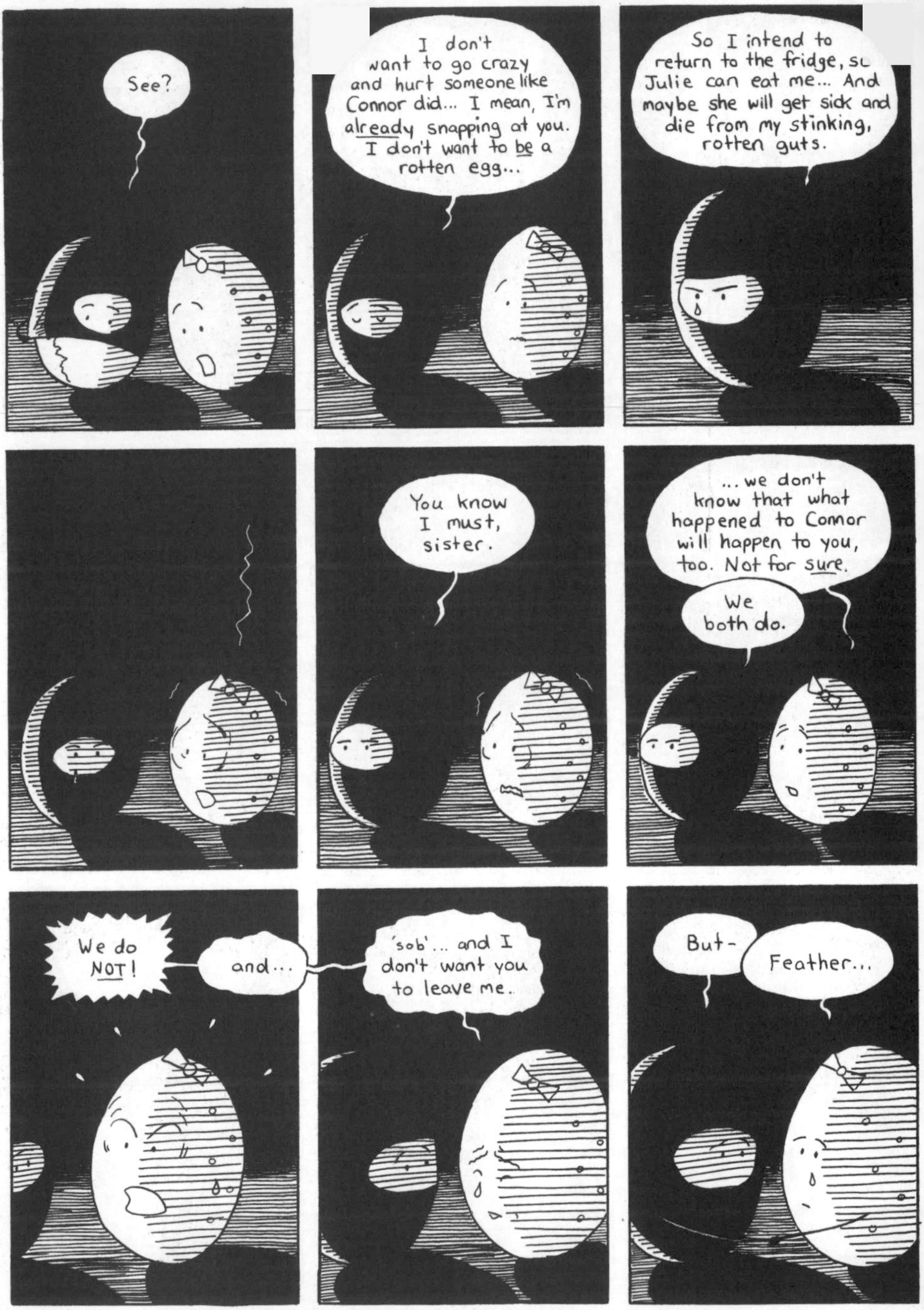
See?
I don't want to go crazy and hurt someone like Connor did... I mean, I'm already snapping at you. I don't want to be a rotten egg...
So I intend to return to the fridge, so Julie can eat me... And maybe she will get sick and die from my stinking, rotten guts.
You know I must, sister.
...we don't know that what happened to Connor will happen to you, too. Not for sure.
We both do.
We do NOT!
and...
'sob'... and I don't want you to leave me..
But-
Feather...

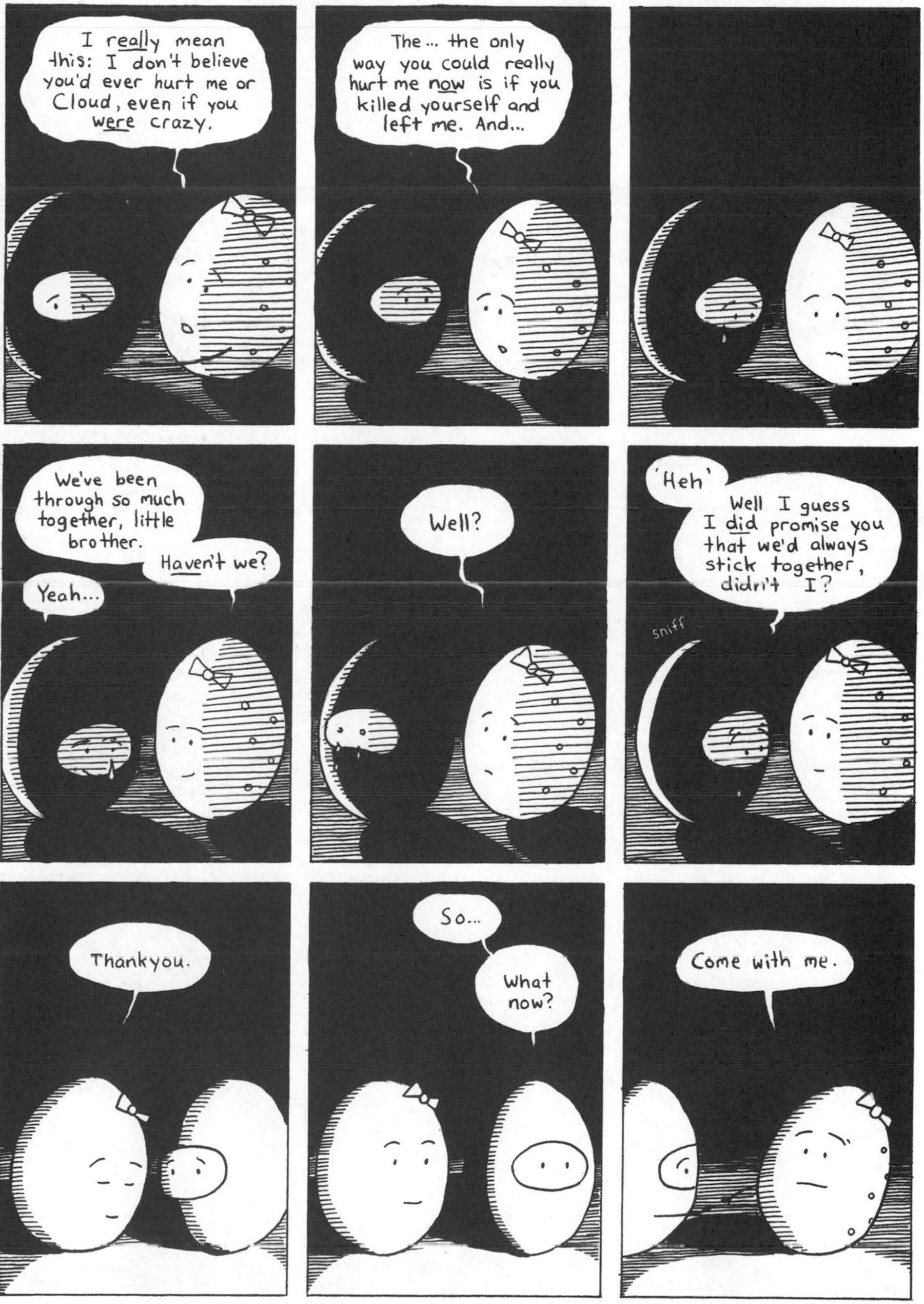
I really mean this: I don't believe you'd ever hurt me or Cloud, even if you were crazy.
The... the only way you could really hurt me now is if you killed yourself and left me. And...
We've been through so much together, little brother.
Haven't we?
Yeah...
Well?
'Heh'
Well I guess I did promise you that we'd always stick together, didn't I?
sniff
Thankyou.
So...
What now?
Come with me.

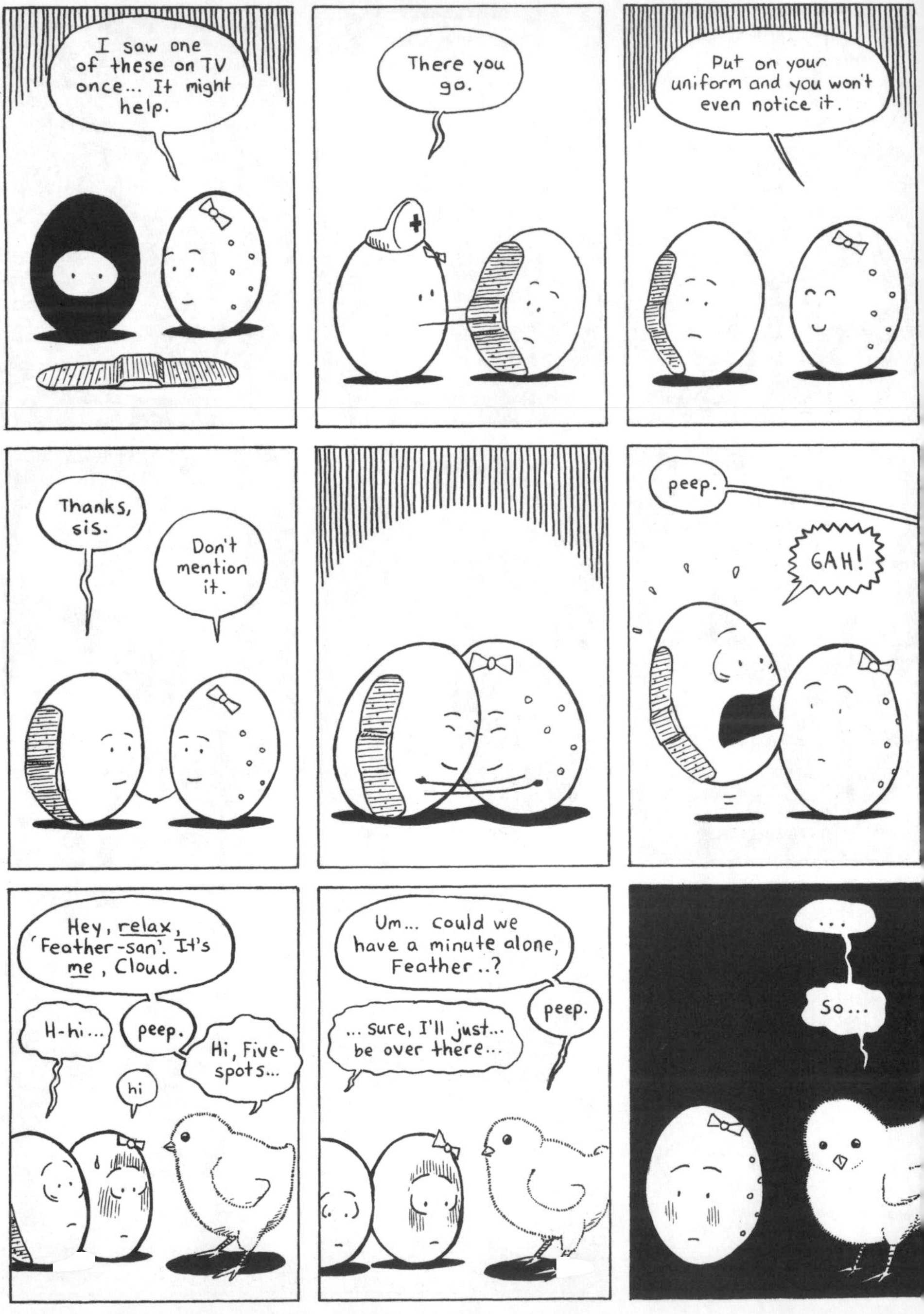

I saw one of these on TV once... It might help.
There you go.
Put on your uniform and you won't even notice it.
Thanks, sis.
Don't mention it.
peep.
GAH!
Hey, relax, 'Feather-san'. It's me, Cloud.
H-hi...
peep.
Hi, Five-spots...
hi
Um... could we have a minute alone, Feather..?
peep.
... sure, I'll just... be over there...
...
So...

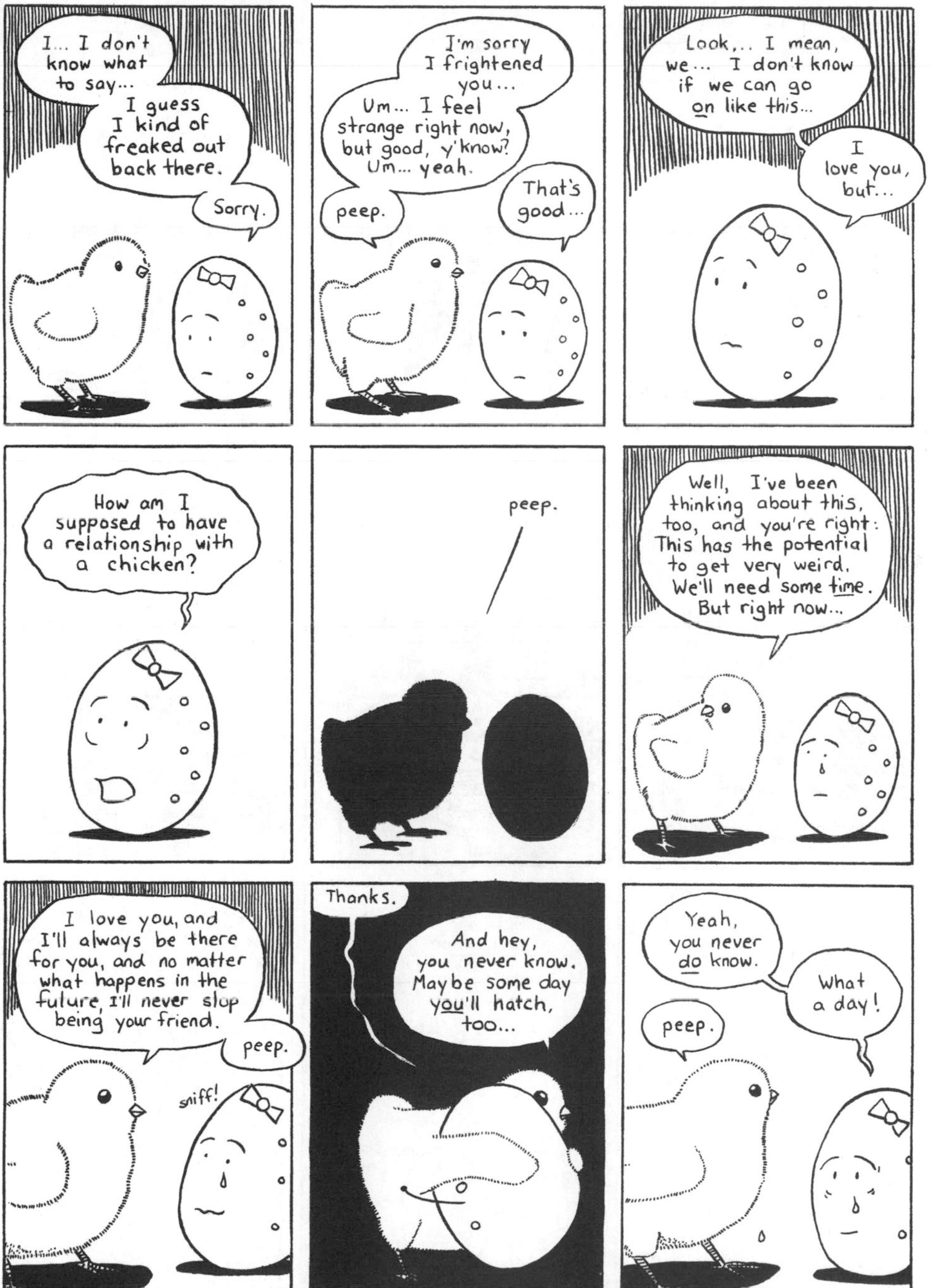

I... I don't know what to say...
I guess I kind of freaked out back there.
Sorry.
I'm sorry I frightened you...
Um... I feel strange right now, but good, y'know? Um... yeah.
peep.
That's good...
Look,... I mean, we... I don't know if we can go on like this...
I love you, but...
How am I supposed to have a relationship with a chicken?
peep.
Well, I've been thinking about this, too, and you're right: This has the potential to get very weird. We'll need some time. But right now...
I love you, and I'll always be there for you, and no matter what happens in the future, I'll never stop being your friend.
peep.
sniff!
Thanks.
And hey, you never know. Maybe some day you'll hatch, too...
Yeah, you never do know.
What a day!
peep.

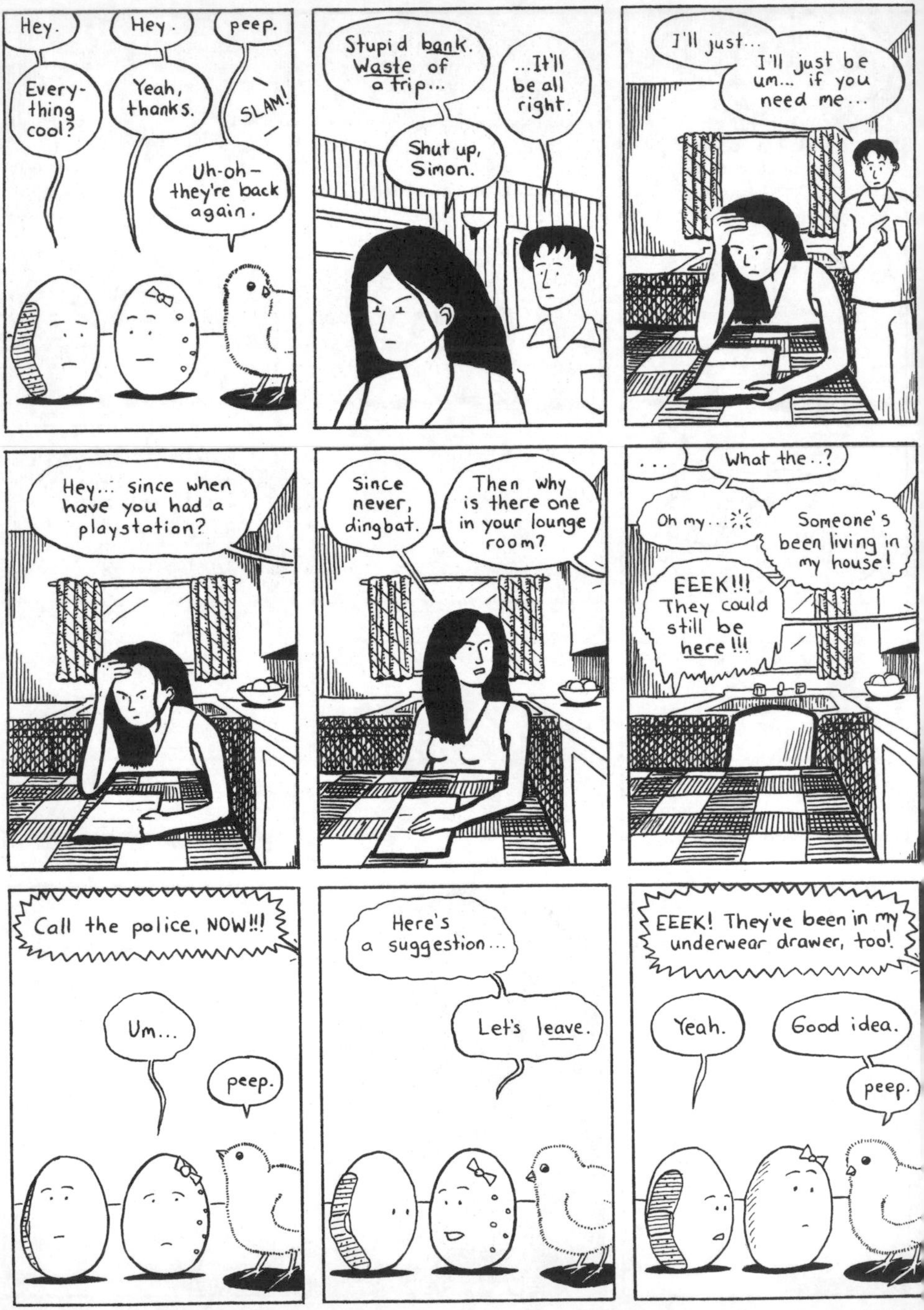
Hey.
Hey.
peep.
Every-thing cool?
Yeah, thanks.
SLAM!
Uh-oh – they're back again.
Stupid bank. Waste of a trip...
...It'll be all right.
Shut up, Simon.
I'll just...
I'll just be um... if you need me...
Hey... since when have you had a playstation?
Since never, dingbat.
Then why is there one in your lounge room?
...
What the..?
Oh my...
Someone's been living in my house!
EEEK!!! They could still be here!!!
Call the police, NOW!!!
Um...
peep.
Here's a suggestion...
Let's leave.
EEEK! They've been in my underwear drawer, too!
Yeah.
Good idea.
peep.